BIKER BILLY'S

ROADHOUSE COOKBOOK

Adventures in Roadside Cuisine

BILL HUFNAGLE

THE LYONS PRESS
GUILFORD, CONNECTICUT
An imprint of The Globe Pequot Press

The Lyons Press is an imprint of The Globe Pequot Press.

Text design by Libby Kingsbury

Photo credits: cover and p. iii, Stevie Senn; pp. x, xvii, 186, 204, 210, 218, Sarah K. Nix;
pp. 207, 209, © Shutterstock.com

All spot illustrations © Shutterstock.com

Library of Congress Cataloging-in-Publication Data is available on file.

ISBN 978-1-59921-434-4

Printed in the United States of America

10 9 8 7 6 5 4 3 2 1

This book is dedicated to Dr. Kim Walters OD PA, Dr. W. Copley McLean Jr., M.D., and Thomas L. Beardsley, M.D. Their exceptional care and gifted efforts saved the sight in my right eye and protected and preserved the sight in my left eye, thus allowing me to continue to enjoy life, work, and riding motorcycles, and to see the daily miracles of God's creations and the people He works those miracles through.

Contents

Foreword

Asking me to write a foreword to a book about food is a pretty tricky proposition, considering that my stomach often guides my way. I figured I would have to travel around the country, stop at all those places Biker Billy talks about, and try the recipes where they originated. These establishments are the real American eateries, where there is pride of ownership and personal service, not like Denny's or Waffle House. Unfortunately I could not get the book's publisher to agree to pay my expenses for the trip.

However, *Biker Billy's Roadhouse Cookbook* is a cookbook, not just a list of roadhouses around the country where you can get good food. Were I less lazy and better with a frying pan I could stay at home and whip up all those recipes myself, but in truth I would rather have somebody else do it for me.

My wife is a good cook, and we have a long row of cookbooks, from *Joy of Cooking* to the delightfully different *The Art of the Cuisine,* illustrated by Toulouse-Lautrec. I have always liked the latter's recipe for "Saint on the Grill," in which the fellow being cooked, ". . . if he is a real saint, he himself will ask to be turned over in order to be grilled to a turn on both sides."

I eat well at home, and Sue has learned that when the two of us are dining alone she serves from the kitchen . . . because if she puts the big dish of food on the table, I will inevitably eat too much. And she does put the gastronomical brakes on when called for. Showing her Frank Sodolak's recipe for chicken-fried bacon, I asked if she could turn out a half dozen rashers so I can determine its worthiness. "Only after I get written permission from your cardiologist," she replied.

The recipes are not overly complicated, since this is not five-star *haute* cuisine, but regular food that regular people cook and regular folk eat. I am tempted to try to make the sausage casserole that The Dillard House in Dillard, Georgia, is noted for. Like any good family man, Billy also includes some recipes by relations, and I found the mac and cheese recipe by his father-in-law, Pop Senn, promising to be quite delicious. Yes, I can whip up a mac and cheese when required.

This is not just a book about food, but also about roads, as Biker Billy throws in a lot of information about American highways and byways, and the roadhouses, their origins and history. It's a pleasure to sit down and read especially if Sue is in the kitchen fixing Tony Packo's Hungarian stuffed cabbage.

—Clement Salvadori

Preface

This book is more than just a collection of highway recipes. If you have read any of my previous cookbooks or my magazine writings, you know that I am a passionate motorcycle rider and chef, in that order. For me, cooking is an expression of the joy of being alive, and I approach it with the same gusto that I approach riding a motorcycle. In fact, I see many parallels between cooking and riding, from the way that great food engages all your senses, just like riding a motorcycle does, to the way that both cooking and riding are activities that you cannot fake having an ability in. And while they are both wonderful when shared with folks you love or at least like a lot, they are both done best as a individual endeavor. Lastly, all food tastes better and is enjoyed more after a long motorcycle ride. If you are a rider, what I just said was pretty clear. For those of you who have never ridden, I will explain.

Good food tastes good when you eat it, nothing more, nothing less, whereas great food first attracts your attention with the sounds and aroma of its cooking. Then, after your mouth begins to water, the food will focus your interest with vibrant or rich colors that attract and hold the eye. Next, the first bite will delight your taste buds. Lastly, the textures will create an engaging mouthfeel that will demand another bite and a deeper exploration of the subtle flavoring. Riding a motorcycle through beautiful countryside will similarly engage all your senses. The sound of the engine as it revs up and down in response to changing road conditions makes music for your soul. Each change in the scenery is accompanied by a new smell, whether it is fresh cut grass or the clean smell of diving into the cool scented air of a pine forest. Every new horizon is painted with different colors from God's palette, from "purple mountain majesty to amber waves of grain," and each beckons you onward to discover what lies over the next rise. As the weather changes you can often smell things like rain falling on the road ahead, and then in what may be an instant or several minutes, you can taste those first drops that land on your lips. Lastly, you feel everything from the ever-changing texture of the pavement to the varying temperatures of the air between sunlit and shaded areas. All five senses come alive with the experiences delivered by both great

food and motorcycling. A car, on the other hand, will get you from here to there, nothing more, nothing less.

You simply can't fake great food. You might make it smell good as it cooks or generate great sounds of sizzle in the pan. You might even go so far as to make it look good sitting on the plate. But the proof is in the tasting. Without a great recipe, top-quality ingredients, and skillful preparation, it will just disappoint in the eating. It is the same with riding—you simply cannot fake it with a motorcycle. If you go out there and try to ride without first getting proper training and developing your knowledge and skills based on a proven program like the one the Motorcycle Safety Foundation teaches, the road will eat you. The same applies if you ride beyond your skills and abilities. That is why although a motorcycle ride is so much more fun when shared with fellow riders; you must ride your own ride. If the rider you are following is more experienced and proficient than you and takes a corner hard and fast, don't try to do it like him. Take the road at your own pace, and ride within what is known as the "envelope of your own skills." Experienced riders know the truth in the expression "the more you know, the better it gets." So get some training.

With that clear, let's return to the subject of road food and the road.

One of the great parts of riding a motorcycle is the adventure of traveling to places unknown, the exploration of the land just over the horizon, the process of seeking new roads, new sights, and—yes, let's face it—new food! Riding builds a very good appetite. The appetite is never the same when traveling the same distance in a car as on a motorcycle. It could be because it's too easy to sit in a car and be entertained much like on one's sofa—with iPod-driven car stereos, satellite radios, cell phones, and even in-car DVD video systems, the family auto is as much an entertainment center as the family living room. Ensconced in the modern roadgoing sofa, it is so easy to nosh while driving and do what our mothers always warned us about—ruin our appetites.

But riding a motorcycle nurtures a good appetite less by making it hard to eat junk food and more by the enchanted method of traveling upon one. Yes, enchanting it is to travel by two-wheeler, to become one with the roads and immersed in the scenery, to fly low along the nape of the earth while swimming in the scents and the changing feel of the air, to partake of the nature of those greener pastures just over the next rise of the road. Motorcycle travel is travel under a magic spell, different as night and day from

blasting past the world encased in a steel-and-glass bubble, seated on your sofa, blissfully distracted by your entertainment. Is it any wonder that riding a motorcycle will build a better appetite than driving?

We who adventure by two wheels are always on the lookout for a great new place to satisfy that enhanced appetite. I am sure some of you have been out there on roads heretofore unexplored, riding until the end of the day's light, gathering every mile and experience you can. At last it is time to find the repast that you have earned so well. But where do you eat? It sure would be nice, in a place you have never been, to know the best spot for a biker to finish off that killer appetite. If you only had riding buddies who had explored the area to clue you in to the best friendly eateries, and, even more important, the best dish at that eatery to experience the chef's pièce de résistance.

> One of the great parts of riding a motorcycle is the process of seeking new roads, new sights, and —yes, let's face it—new food!

That is where I hope this book will be of service to you. I have reached out to my many friends and readers in the motorcycle community and asked them for recommendations on great eateries hidden along their favorite local rides or in their hometowns. I have also added some from the beautiful area I call home, the Blue Ridge Mountains of western North Carolina, where you will find some of the premiere riding roads in America. Local folks tend to know the consistently good places to eat, and these are often not the restaurants closest to the highway with the flashiest signs. The one hundred or so recipes in this book represent a sampling of what is out there to be discovered just past the neon glare. In this one book I could never include every great eatery on every great road in America. But the folks who recommended them prize the ones in here.

At the start of this preface I said that this book is more than just a collection of highway recipes. I feel that you, my dear reader, will find the enclosed road food recipes and road food in general more enjoyable if you know a little more about from whence they came, if you know something of the great adventurous stories of how our road system—truly a modern wonder and the envy of the world—came to be what it is today, and through that knowledge

gain some perspective on how our food culture evolved alongside those roads. But this is also, as I first stated, primarily a cookbook, so I have endeavored to give you what I would call "history light." You will not be burdened with footnotes and citations from obscure tomes and dusty documents. Rather, I prefer to spin you a tale much like I would share it with you as a conversation over a glass of fine old Kentucky bourbon—assuming, of course, the bikes were parked for the night. Drinking and the road just don't make a good recipe.

In the following pages of this book you will find an introduction that should give you some sense of who I am and why this is a book I wanted to write. You will find a chapter on the history of the American road and motorized travel, which also relates the rise, decline, and rebirth of the uniquely local roadside eateries, typically mom-and-pop operations. Sprinkled throughout the book are snapshots of historic roads, iconic restaurant chains, and some other colorful things.

It is my sincere hope that this book will inspire your own personal journey to discover America one roadhouse at a time. To perhaps spend some winter evenings reading more on our cultural history, not the history of big-city highfalutin society, but of the regular Joe and Jane Doe who built and lived in the heartland. Maybe you will cook some of these recipes, share them with friends, and tell some tales of the road. You might even plan your next road trip to include stops at the establishments that graciously shared their cherished recipes with us.

I have a personal saying that I have espoused over the years: "Life is too short to eat dull food." So get out there and find new places along the road that will serve you exciting foods! Then share them with all your friends and me.

Introduction:
Roads Run through It

I love to travel, see new places, meet new folks, and, of course, eat at different places along the way. These days my busy touring schedule has me racking up airline miles like mad, and I do enjoy flying—after all, it is really the only way to get to truly distant places like Australia, Europe, and Hawaii. But flying is all about the destination, and this is not my preferred way of approaching life. Life is about the journey. All the real fun is in the adventures you have along the way to your destination, and indeed a destination is not even necessary to have great travel fun. A lot of my most enjoyable journeys have been the ones where I set off knowing only that I have to be back by a certain date. I inspect and pack the bike during the week before my trip, and then, when the much-anticipated morning of departure arrives, I roll the bike out of the garage. A last safety check and a brief effort to remember the thing that I have surely forgotten to pack—I always forget something—and then it is time to fire up the motor, mount the bike, and ride. It is within the first few minutes of the trip that I decide which direction to head. From there it is turn by turn, back road by back road, meal by meal, and by the whim of the front wheel that a trip begins to reveal itself. On those rides, the where I am going matters less than the simple act of traveling; perhaps it is because I am answering the call of my wanderlust. I truly love to travel by road—road-tripping rocks—especially when done by motorcycle. You just can't explore like that by plane or train.

But more often than not, life has places to get to and schedules to keep. While exploring may sound like an impractical way to travel to a destination and keep to a schedule, it can work. Just keep pointed in the correct general direction and stay off the main routes of travel, and you will rediscover America and find lots of great and memorable sights, people, and places to eat along the way. More time will likely be needed, but more value and memories will be received in return. It was the way I learned to travel as a child. I remember adults, when speaking of my father, saying he never took the same way twice.

It is a way of approaching travel that is now ingrained into my being. But it has evolved into more than just a habitual way of approaching the act of traveling: It is a defining part of who I am.

Among my fondest memories from childhood are the ones that spring from road trips to Mammaw's house in the mountains of eastern Tennessee. Our yearly family vacations were spent visiting family down home in those hills. For those of you unfamiliar with the affectionate and familiar names of the south, Mammaw was my mother's mother; she would have been called Grandma or Granny if she had been from the north. Thankfully, she was a great lady of the South, a native of North Carolina who had migrated west to the wild hills of eastern Tennessee as small child in the late 1800s. I say thankfully not just because I value my southern roots, which I do greatly (though I am also in part a child of the big city). Rather, I am thankful because those family vacations were bookended by long road trips. Many of those road trips were traveled in the days before the new road, in this case Interstate 81, bypassed the old roads and before so many of the delightfully unique roadside places faded away. Actually, I am doubly thankful because those road trips passed through some of the most beautiful mountains and valleys in the eastern states—primarily the Blue Ridge Mountains and the Shenandoah Valley, a region filled with the history of our great nation and its struggles to define itself.

Those long road trips were necessary because we—Mom, Dad, and me—lived in the South Bronx, the area where my father's family had called home from the time they immigrated to America from Europe generations before. New York City was my childhood home, the other end of those road trips and therefore one of the two root places in my family tree. This gave me an upbringing that was divided between sometimes polar opposites, which made for really great learning experiences. During my childhood I was able to develop both an appreciation for the quiet of the country and the energy of the big city. Along with this I developed a deeply ingrained love of the road and all the adventures that it holds, especially the culinary ones.

Among the strong childhood memories from the Bronx were the times we spent in the Cosmos Restaurant. This small local eatery sat on the corner of East Tremont Avenue and Clinton Avenue, half a block from our apartment. (It is still there, almost half a century later and I would have loved to get a recipe from them to share with you, but alas I could never make contact with

the current owners.) We gathered there with members of our extended family, sometimes filling several booths. The Cosmos was in many ways an extension of our family dining room; we ate there often and shared family social times. It was always a treat. I also remember the smell of coffee roasting in the morning air on the walk to the school bus stop, and the sound of the Maxwell House coffee percolator jingle on the radio in our kitchen during breakfast. The sweets at the neighborhood ice cream parlor, buttered popcorn at the movies, and especially Mom's home cooking were among the simple delights of the childhood days in the Bronx. It wouldn't be until years later, as a young adult, that I discovered the true bounty of dining in the big city and developed my love for foods from diverse world cultures. But enough of those later years for now; let's return back to my bifurcated roots and the road.

In Tennessee, my mother's family lived up the same holler they had settled in at the end of the nineteenth century. By the time of my earliest memories, they had built a then-new house, moving just down along the hillside, and selling the old house to kin. I don't really remember the old house, but that new house is strong in my memories. If you saw it now as it was in the 1960s, it would seem more like a museum exhibit of early Appalachian Mountain frontier living rather than a contemporary suburban home of that era. However, that house was still in use during my childhood and all the way through my young adulthood. The kitchen had a large wood-burning cookstove with two ovens that Mammaw baked the most wonderful biscuits in. It also featured a modern convenience that the old house lacked, running water, one temperature only, from a hand pump at the kitchen sink. That was the extent of indoor plumbing. There was a two-seater just down the hill; actually, it had two extra seats of kid height, a fact my aunt Joyce reminded me about recently. The house was built with wide plank floors, a tin roof, and an unpainted exterior. Below the house on the downhill side was what some might call a basement. Actually it was an earthen cellar lined with shelves where Mammaw stored her home-canned foods. That storage cellar was a cool, dark, wonderful place for kids to sneak into on a hot southern summer day. It was also a good place to get into trouble if you broke one of Mammaw's jars, which contained valuable food, grown and stored by hard work for feeding the family during the coming winter. Reached by dirt roads over steep hills along a winding hollow, Mammaw's place was a truck farm where she grew or raised almost everything the family ate, except for things

like flour and sugar. It was a quiet place, except for us kids running, yelling, and enjoying the barefoot freedom of summer. It was a great safe place to spend childhood summers. It was also a place of deep connection for me. Connection to a bygone time when people lived closer to the land, closer to where food came from—it is a connection that I value highly. That was a simpler time and place.

Back in the Bronx, we lived in a railroad flat, in an apartment building on East Tremont Avenue. My room was the one at the back end of the apartment. One window of my room faced toward the Cross-Bronx Expressway, which was about two blocks away. It was to the lullaby of cars and trucks cruising along that sunken urban roadway that I slept at night. The sounds of engines roaring and tires singing on the road were the quiet sounds of the city, which were often punctuated by sirens and garbage trucks in the night. As I slept, that sound of the road filled my dreams. It is little wonder that my favorite toys both then and now are motorcycles and cars. That road was also the first road of my earliest remembered family trips. While we actually started on local city streets before we entered the expressway, it was at the expressway entrance that true road trips began in that era of my childhood. The Cross-Bronx Expressway led us to the George Washington Bridge over the Hudson River and into the country. It was a big fast road as seen through the eyes of childhood, and it was the start of adventures, even if that was only a visit to a closer family member in New Jersey. I was born the same year that Eisenhower signed the Federal Highway Act of 1956, which created the interstates and helped to fund the completion of the Cross-Bronx Expressway. While that expressway today is old, worn, and woefully too small for the traffic it carries, in the days of my early childhood it was a new road—bigger, faster, and busier than the rest of the roads we followed on the trips we took back then. The transition from big urban highways to small country roads was symbolic of the escape from the hustle and bustle of the shoe-bound days of the urban school year to the barefoot peaceful play of the mountains.

It is ironic that the year my life started was the year that rang the death knell for the old roads that I love so much. It was my beginning—and the beginning of the end for many of the great historic roads and the communities, businesses, and lifestyles that prospered along those roads. As I write this, looking back on that dichotomy in my lifetime, I also know it was the realization of a dream that started almost a century ago. You will find out

about that dream and how it created the life cycle of the American road and food culture in the some of the following chapters.

Another ironic and personally very sad milestone occurred while I was writing this introduction.

My cell phone rang the other day, a rather common occurrence. The caller ID showed a nonlocal number; this is also rather common. My work brings me calls from all over the country. But this was an uncommon and sad call—it was my aunt Joyce telling me that my aunt Devota had died. She had fallen and broken her femur just above the knee, and during the surgery to stabilize the break she had had a heart attack, and then another post-op. It was the second one that took her. Devota was almost ninety years old; she had lived a good long life and had lived it well. Although in recent years I hadn't seen her often, I will miss her dearly. Joyce is now the last survivor of almost twenty aunts and uncles. In another way, though, Devota's passing marks the end of an era.

She was my late mother's closest sister, in both age and life's journey. She was also the last fellow traveler from the days of my childhood. It was with her and her husband, Uncle Bunk, that Mom and I took the summer road trips that in so many ways shaped my life. Back in those days we traveled together to Mammaw's place in the mountains of eastern Tennessee. Mom would drive us down from New Jersey along Interstate 95 to Baltimore, where Bunk and Devota lived. We would spend the night at their house and make ready for the journey the next day. That was always an evening of excitement and anticipation. At dawn we would be off along a route that varied some each year—there would be new things to see, places to stop and eat, souvenir shops to explore, motels with pools to swim in, and at the end of two or three days of traveling, Mammaw's place awaited us. These were the road trips that instilled the wanderlust and love of the road that shaped who I am.

It was too late for me to get an affordable flight to Baltimore, so I would have to drive there from my North Carolina home. I could only be gone for two days—just enough to drive up, attend the evening viewing and the next morning's funeral, then drive back again. Since this was late January, with a winter storm moving east through Ohio, riding back-to-back 500-mile days would not be too wise. I rented a car, MapQuested the route to the funeral parlor, and set out for Baltimore.

The computer-generated route took me north over the mountains into Tennessee and along Interstate 81 to Winchester, Virginia, then east through Harpers Ferry, along Interstate 70 onto the 695 beltway, and finally into the part of Baltimore where Bunk and Devota had lived for so many years. A thousand miles of driving, even filled with an iPod's worth of music, gives one a lot of time to reflect. As I drove north along I-81, the many place-names and route numbers on the exit signs and the billboards took me back in time. I was traveling in reverse order much the same route that Devota, Bunk, Mom, and I had made so many times during my childhood.

These were the road trips that instilled the wanderlust and love of the road that shaped who I am.

Together we had traveled the many roads that traverse this part of the country: from the Blue Ridge Parkway on top of the mountains, down to the valley floor along U.S. Highway 11 (in places still called "the Lee Highway"), and along the many other roads that crisscross between the old-time tourist attractions. When I was little we traveled them all. Then came the new road, I-81, and we traveled that, too. As the years rolled by, we took those trips less often.

After I had grown and started to take motorcycle vacations, I often rode down and back on the Blue Ridge Parkway, a personal favorite escape from my New York City life then. Close to a decade ago, when I moved to North Carolina, I drove the big moving truck south on I-81 though the Shenandoah Valley, which since then has become my roadway of choice when I drive to and from the northeast.

In so many ways, the roads up and down those mountains and through that valley are the roadways of my life, which I came to understand as I drove home from the funeral with pictures of Devota, Bunk, and Mammaw on the front passenger seat. While Mammaw and the family aren't waiting in the hills for our visit, Mom, Devota, and Bunk have all joined her in a far better place. I will always have them traveling with me in my heart till this narrow winding road leads me home to join them.

1

You Can't Get There from Here: A History of the American Road

Road food would not exist without the American highway, the vehicles that ply them, and the people who travel along them. It is sometimes hard to imagine from the vantage point of our contemporary society, where driving to work or the store or cross-country is a common occurrence, that a little less than a century ago these activities were at best only a dream. Today any vehicle on the road that is well maintained according to the manufacturer's specifications and able to pass state inspection could reliably travel from coast to coast and back again with little more service needed than an oil change. On that cross-country round-trip the travelers would rarely be more than a dozen miles (often less) from all the modern conveniences and services they expect at home. True, there are still sections of the western states where the distances between communities are larger than a dozen miles, but even there you would be hard-pressed (but not unable) to find a place that was more than a half hour's drive along the interstate from a gas station, hotel, or restaurant.

During the first decade of the last century, things were very different for travelers. Automobiles and motorcycles were just beginning to transition from the realm of playthings for wealthy enthusiasts and hobbyists to viable mass-market products. That decade saw the transformation of these products from the highly diverse creations of a multitude of inventors and backyard tinkers into relatively standardized design configurations that we easily recognize as the forebears of our modern motorcycles and cars. During those exciting years of the invention of motorized vehicles, many of the great marquees, which are household names today, were founded. Of course, hundreds of fledgling enterprises whose pioneering efforts positively impacted the development and maturation of motorized vehicles, and whose names were well known in those days, failed to survive the turbulent times since then.

While cars and motorcycles were beginning to prove themselves as viable means of conveyance and were a development of much interest and excitement to the public, there was little in the way of infrastructure to support their common usage. Paved roads were basically nonexistent, except in the larger cities. What rural roads that did exist beyond those cities were not much more than wagon trails or horse paths that mostly followed what had once been animal traces or Indian trails. For the most part, roads of that day did not constitute a connected network that allowed easy direct travel from city to city, let alone coast to coast. Most roads were impassable by early motor vehicles during rainy times or the winter months. Road maintenance, when done at all, was usually the work of the farmer whose land the road crossed, and that road was used primarily to bring his product to market. Motorized vehicles rarely traveled much farther than their horse-powered predecessors did in a day's time. It would be fair to say that

> While cars and motorcycles were beginning to prove themselves as viable means of conveyance and were a development of much interest and excitement to the public, there was little in the way of infrastructure to support their common usage.

except for the folks who were part of the waning days of America's westward migration, travel of more than a few days' distance was the exception, not the norm for the average American. When they did travel a long distance it was usually by railroad, often with nonmotorized conveyances providing the connection between the rail lines and remote locations.

Yet the lack of roads did not stop intrepid adventurers from motoring across the continent. In 1903 Dr. Horatio Nelson Jackson and a young mechanic named Sewall K. Crocker became the first people to successfully make a transcontinental journey by automobile. They started their adventure in San Francisco on May 23rd and arrived in New York City on July 26th, taking just over two months (sixty-four days) to make the journey. However, they were not the first to motor across the continent. Slightly earlier that same year, George A. Wyman made the journey from San Francisco to New York City on a single-cylinder motorcycle. He did it in less than two months (fifty-one days), starting out in San Francisco on May 16th and arriving in New York City on July 6th. These daring fellows were celebrities of the day and received tremendous coverage in the nation's newspapers. But they were not the only noteworthy achievers of that year; 1903 was truly a watershed year in transportation history. Within the span of those twelve months, many firsts were achieved, notably among them: The Ford Motor Company was incorporated; William Harley and the Davidson brothers Arthur, Walter, and William began producing iconic motorcycles; and the Wright Brothers, Wilbur and Orville, flew the first airplane.

The same year, some interesting things were happening in the world of food. The first U.S. patent was issued for instant coffee, and the Pepsi-Cola trademark was registered. James Beard was born; he was to become a true icon in the culinary world. Legend has it that the club sandwich was first made during that year. Tuna was canned for the first time, and Richard Hellmann created his famous recipe for bottled mayonnaise. For the most part, all were very promising starts. But road food as we know it today was still a thing of the future, even though America's first restaurant chain was in its third decade of operation. The Harvey Houses had been providing a fine dining experience to railroad travelers at water stops and stations along the Atchison, Topeka and Santa Fe Railway since the mid-1880s.

As the first decade of the last century ended and motor vehicles assumed the pathway of inexorable destiny that made them one of the transformative forces of the twentieth century, the lack of a network of roads was the one thing that could have stopped that progress. Yet there was no organized public effort to develop roads. Beyond the captains of the industries who built vehicles, parts, and accessories and refined fuel and oil, there was little public interest in roads. That would all change thanks to the pioneering adventures of motor enthusiasts and a handful of road visionaries.

Birth of the American Road—*Are We There Yet?*

As the decade of the teens dawned, there were approximately two and a half million miles of mostly rutted dirt roads in America. Roads led basically nowhere, most emanating in settled communities and wandering outward till they petered out in some farmer's field. Precious few led to another town or community. While paving of various forms had been known since the Roman times, there had been little of it done in America beyond a few gravel or watered-bonded macadam roads from the horse-drawn-stagecoach era. Those early paved roads were really only suitable for horses and wagons, not for the weight and speed of motorized vehicles. A notable exception was a strip of Pennsylvania Avenue paved with asphalt bonded by naturally occurring pitch from the island of Trinidad; this was done in 1876 at the request of then-president Grant. But all that was about to change.

There was another strip of pavement, made of crushed stone and tar, that would play a much more important role in birthing America's roads than that Pennsylvania Avenue asphalt. The Indianapolis Motor Speedway, which was founded in 1909 and hosted its first motor race on August 14th of that year, was the vision of a gentleman named Carl Fisher. Fisher, one of the four founders of the Indianapolis Motor Speedway, was a man of big ideas and visions. An interesting side note is that the first race was a motorcycle race; automobiles took the track for the first time on August 19th. After the first automobile race the track surface was deemed unsafe. It was replaced with 3.2 million bricks in time for a race in December that was canceled due to below-freezing temperatures. The achievements of the first decade of the twentieth century saw motorcycles getting there first, in both cross-country records and in racing. But it would be in the teens that the race to road-up America would start in earnest. Just like he did with racing at the Brick Yard, Carl Fisher would be at the wheel of both.

Carl Fisher's Dream

In 1912, the year that Carl Fisher made the Indy 500 the world's highest-paying sporting event, he also had a dream. A dream of a graveled road crossing the continent from New York to San Francisco, it was a $10 million dream. He had hoped to pay for it mostly from a voluntary contribution of 1 percent of revenues from the expanding motor industries. He almost got it, too, but Henry Ford balked, feeling that if the industry paid for road improvements, the public never would. Without Henry Ford's support, the industry did not follow. Funny, if you think about it, 1 percent is a lot less than anybody pays for road taxes. However, all was not lost for Carl Fisher's dream. Two brave titans of the industry supported him: Henry Joy, the president of Packard, and Frank Seiberling, the president of Goodyear. Their money and efforts would prove vital, but it was not then, nor ever, enough money to pay for building the road—especially not in time for their stated goal of having the road open by 1915, just in time for the Panama-Pacific Exposition scheduled to be held in San Francisco that year.

Having achieved enthusiastic interest from the public and searching for a way to inspire Congress to fund it, Henry Joy hit upon the idea of naming the road after Abraham Lincoln. At the same time, Congress was debating spending $1.7 million on the Lincoln Memorial. Guess what happened? It is a great monument. They named the proposed road the Lincoln Highway and formed the Lincoln Highway Association, which was active until 1925. They managed to lay out a route, pave parts of it with concrete, and inspire the nation. As the decade of the teens rolled on, folks traveled the road. Some made it to the 1915 Panama-Pacific Exposition. Among the folks who journeyed the road in that decade was a young lady writer named Emily Post. That's right, the very same Emily Post who became famous for writing *the* book on etiquette in 1922. She actually did not follow the entire Lincoln Highway route on her journey in 1915 to the exposition. Rumor of construction on the road in the western Pennsylvania mountains made her party choose to go north via Buffalo, Cleveland, and Chicago, where they rejoined the Lincoln Highway. Dear Emily, a lady of society, only agreed to take the journey and write about it for *Collier's Weekly* as long as she would be able to stay in the finest hotels with fine dining rooms. By Chicago she was ready to accept the reality of camping and cooking on the road. She was not going to let the experience of a lifetime escape her. She, like the thousands who traveled the Lincoln Highway coast to coast in that decade, had to rough it at least some of the time. In those days road food was still a thing of the future. Meals were acquired at overnight stops, whether in fancy hotels in the larger cities or in less-luxurious inns in small towns. As one traveled farther west, accommodations and meals were to be found at ranches and farmsteads, some of which, as the road traffic grew, made a good portion of their yearly income by stocking goods and catering to the needs of travelers. The tourist trade was born.

Along with tourists came the first tourist traps. There was at least one actual physical trap designed to ensnare the early motor vehicles. Along the route of the Lincoln Highway between Salt Lake City and Ely, Nevada, one would pass through Fish Springs. This route loosely followed the old Pony Express route, and Fish Springs had been a way station for it and the Overland Stage. The route passed on the south side of the great salt desert. A colorful character well known in the road lore of the day was John Thomas. He was described as living the life of a hermit in the old Fish Springs Express Station, yet he also provided meals, lodging, fuel, oil, and a horse-powered towing service. Legend has it that the Lincoln Highway had a fork in the road a distance east of Thomas's place, one fork appearing to travel directly through a salt marsh, and the other taking a longer high-ground route around the marsh. Those who chose the direct route soon found themselves on a stretch of very rough and rutted road, although the ground on either side looked smooth and solid. Here lay the trap. Once one ventured off the road, the car would break through the salt crust surface and get completely stuck. As the legend goes, there was a sign just ahead that read IF IN NEED OF A TOW LIGHT A FIRE, along with material to burn. Shortly thereafter, Mr. Thomas would appear with his tow horses, and one had to pay the hefty tow fee or remain stuck in the desert. Some say that Thomas had diverted a small stream or spring to make the ground always soggy, and that any brief rain shower would erase the signs of the last victim's passage. Whether folklore or fact, the tourist trap was born.

As the years of the teens rolled on, garages and hotels began to sprout up in towns along the Lincoln Highway and other roads. Another phenomenon that also grew during these years was the competition between towns and communities and even states to have the new transcontinental highway and the growing tourist trade routed their way. In 1914 the cross-country road craze took a turn south—north and south, that is—with the formation of the Dixie Highway Association. If you guessed that it sounded like a Carl Fisher idea, you were right. Mr. Fisher was involved in this route, which ultimately ran from Montreal, Canada, to Miami, Florida. A major difference this time was that the competition between cities and towns to be on the official route was so pronounced that the Dixie Highway ended up as two roughly parallel routes with some connector routes between them. Basically it formed, more or less, a network of roads between the northern Midwest and southern Florida. At the time, Miami Beach was not the fabulously rich vacation destination city it is today; rather it was more of a swamp, owned in part by none other than Carl Fisher—perhaps it is the ultimate example of the expression "if you build it, they will come." A year before missing the goal of building a road from coast to coast in time for the 1915 Panama-Pacific Exposition, Carl Fisher had moved on from the Lincoln Highway to the Dixie Highway. It is ironic that 1915 was the fiftieth anniversary of the end of the Civil War, in which President Lincoln successfully preserved the Union, as well as the birth year of a north–south road named the

Dixie Highway, whose western route passes through Hodgenville, Kentucky, where Lincoln was born.

In 1916 two landmark events happened. Woodrow Wilson signed the Federal Aid Road Act of 1916, which led to the first federal funding of road improvements. Also that year, the Van Buren sisters, Augusta and Adeline, were the first women to cross the continent, riding solo on a pair of Indian motorcycles. It should be noted that the Van Buren sisters were not the first women to motor across America. That honor went to Alice Huyler Ramsey in 1909, who drove three female passengers from New York to San Francisco. It is interesting that men set records driving eastward and women driving westward. Before much could be achieved with the monies from the Federal Aid Road Act of 1916, however, America entered World War I on April 16, 1917. The nation turned its attention from building roads at home to winning the "War to End All Wars" in Europe. Within a year of the armistice that hailed the end of the first mechanized war, a convoy composed of military vehicles from several manufacturers left Washington, D.C., and headed for California. Led by a small fleet of civilian vehicles from the automobile industry, they traveled northwest to join the path of the Lincoln Highway. For the Lincoln Highway Association this was a great publicity coup; for the military and the manufacturers seeking to develop vehicles for them, it was a road test of epic proportions. Along their journey to San Francisco they learned much about the need to improve both vehicles and the roads. It was the voice of the military in Congress speaking in the name of national defense that would ultimately lead to the paving of America. A young military man by the name of Eisenhower, who traveled in that experimental convoy, would decades later play a pivotal role in that process.

Uncle Sam Steps In—Let Byways be Highways

As the decade of teens roared into the twenties, Americans increasingly fell in love with the automobile and the road. In 1921 Warren G. Harding became the first president to ride to his inauguration in a car. Later that year he would sign the Federal Highway Act of 1921. The times were changing; motor travel was now affordable by the common man and was not just an extravagance of the wealthy. Henry Ford's Model T sold for less than three hundred dollars in 1926. By the middle of the decade the country was crisscrossed with roads. Yet it was not a true system of roads, but rather a wild collection of roads, many with names that changed as they flowed from place to place. Traveler confusion was common. By the end of 1925 a new system was developed, but only after much compromise between the various state highway officials and the federal government. The new numbered system of federal highways, still in use today, and marked by the federal shield symbol as a background for the route number, was the birth of a new era for the American road landscape. It also was the end of an era. Within two years of the announcement of the new numbered system, the Lincoln Highway Association, a group so influential in promoting good roads for America, ceased to operate. For them, perhaps the ultimate injustice was that their Lincoln Highway was broken up into several different highway route numbers as it crossed the continent. Nineteen twenty-seven was also the year that the Dixie Highway Association disbanded their routes and became various state roads and parts of the new federal system. This was the fate of all the named roads.

Example of Federal Highway Route signs, located at Cheyenne Crossing, South Dakota BILL HUFNAGLE

The end of the twenties saw America with more than eight hundred thousand miles of improved highways. The last year of the decade saw the sale of motor vehicles set record numbers that would not be bested until after World War II. All during this decade, as motor tourism grew, tourist camps sprung up in or on the outskirts of many towns, mostly offering free camping as a means to draw economy-minded travelers into town to buy supplies. While the wealthy still traveled in fancy touring cars, stayed in fine hotels, and applied the lessons of Emily Post's *Etiquette,* most Americans journeyed forth in Model Ts and other similar low-priced cars, camping and cooking out along the way.

October 29, 1929 (aka Black Tuesday), marked the beginning of the Great Depression, resulting in the decade of the thirties beginning on a far different note than the twenties. Motor vehicle travel was now becoming commonplace, and the adventure and excitement of the day had turned skyward as airplanes, zeppelins, and flying filled the public imagination. Charles A. Lindbergh had made his famous nonstop flight from New York to Paris in 1927, and Amelia Earhart made her solo Atlantic crossing in 1932. She set records and generated headlines up until 1937, when she disappeared, the same year that the *Hindenburg* crashed.

Many things disappeared, appeared, or changed in that decade, mostly driven by the economic and agricultural woes. But the roads continued to be ever more crowded. A new migration started as families seeking a better life packed up the family car or truck and headed west. This too was a force that spawned many changes. The tourist camps of the twenties faded away; businesses that once were profitable in towns moved out of town to find both cheaper lands to build on and to attract business from the road. The new numbered highways began to bypass many downtowns as traffic pressures built. While the Joads and the Okies in their jalopies rolled westward and the dust settled on the Great Plains, a new roadscape had begun to appear. This was the era that saw the birth of the legendary roads and road culture perhaps best exemplified by Route 66, "the Mother Road." It was also the era of the New Deal and great road and infrastructure building throughout America. Government agencies like the Civilian Conservation Corps (CCC) and Works Progress Administration (WPA) put the nation to work building what are now historic and scenic icons such as the Blue Ridge Parkway.

The restoring of the economy, rebuilding of the American industry, resettling of the population, and building of new infrastructure continued at a strong pace as the decade of the 1930s ended and the 1940s began. But it all was to change again as December 1941 saw a shocked nation drawn into World War II. The war years saw the rationing of gasoline, tires, and most consumer goods. The automobile and motorcycle manufacturers turned their production toward supplying our brave troops with the tools to fight tyranny. Most companies who could manufacture war goods were pleased to get the contracts, and America's industrial capabilities grew. When the war ended, all that capacity shifted as quickly as possible to peacetime production. The great postwar boom was on. The returning GIs and their new families moved to the new suburbs, and new cars and new roads were the order of the day. This era was the beginning of the true renaissance for the road and for roadside business, including eateries of all description. The peacetime boom that began in the late forties transitioned into the "Happy Days" of the fifties. Along the way, that boom became the baby boom.

One Dream Realized—Many Dreams Bypassed

Business and life were good along America's numbered highways in the late forties and early fifties, but traffic was getting ever more congested and peace more fragile. Dwight David Eisenhower became the thirty-fifth president of the United States in 1953 and served throughout the remainder of that decade. He was at the helm while many things evolved in the

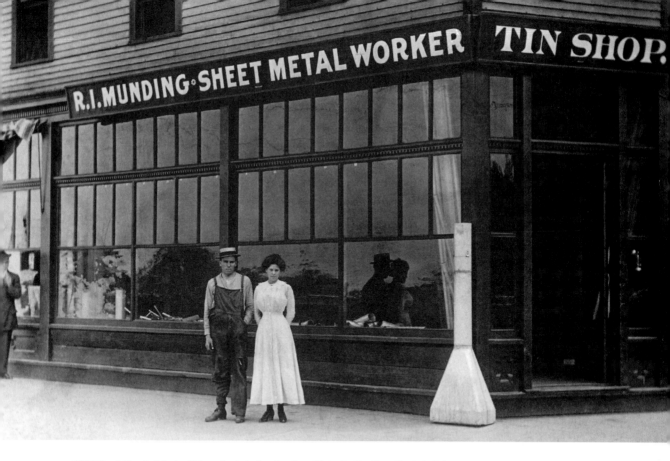

1902 Front Street, Toledo, Ohio, prior to being developed into the first Tony Packo's Cafe TONY PACKO'S CAFÉ

postwar world: the Korean War cease-fire, the developing cold war, the expansion of nuclear weapons as a defense posture, the birth of the space race, and the Interstate Highway System. President Eisenhower signed the Federal-Aid Highway Act of 1956 on June 29, 1956; it was in some ways most ironic. This legislation, which was pushed by Eisenhower, was founded in lessons he learned as a young man on the 1919 Transcontinental Motor Convoy, and upon observations of the German autobahns during and after World War II. Couple those lessons with the cold war theory of Mutual Assured Destruction (MAD), and it was clear to him that we needed a network of controlled access, wide highways that could support the transportation of military resources and evacuate large cities as well as support civilian travel and commerce. In many ways it was the final realization of the dream that Carl Fisher had back in 1912, and it was lobbied for by the automobile industry. The ironic part lies in that Carl Fisher's dream, the Lincoln Highway, was effectively killed by the Federal Highway Act of 1921, which created the system of numbered federal highways. The numbered roads cut up the Lincoln Highway and doomed it to obscurity while giving rise to iconic roads like Route 66. Again ironically, as soon as the ink dried on the Federal-Aid Highway Act of 1956 on June 29, 1956, the death knell had rung for the culture of those iconic roads.

It was an unexpected consequence and a slow wasting death—a great decline—but in many ways it went mostly unnoticed. The new interstate highways were slowly built along the general pathways of the older roads. They bypassed many of the small businesses and communities that had sprung up along the old roads. Yes, you could leave the interstate at the exchanges and reach the old roads, but many of the businesses that had grown up along the old roads were invisible from the new roads; even if you knew they were there, it was almost always an inconvenience to detour to frequent them. Nine years after the Federal-Aid Highway Act of 1956 became law, President Lyndon B. Johnson signed the Highway Beautification Act of 1965. This act removed most signage from the interstate system and effectively removed the last visual reminders that the old road businesses existed.

> The new interstate highways were slowly built along the general pathways of the older roads.

Some businesses moved to the interstate exchanges and survived; even more new businesses flourished at those junctures. Much like the railroads had done at water stops, new towns sprang up along the new roads. It was not that long ago that the era changed from the unique mom-and-pop roadside America to the franchised sameness of the interstate. But, as you will see in the following chapters, the old roads and the old ways did not completely die out, although they had receded almost out of sight. Thankfully they did survive and are experiencing a resurgence of interest: Now we call them the Blue Line Roads, after their color on some maps. Along those blue lines there is still to be found the living history of the American road and the down-home taste of its food.

2

Breakfast

Morning on the road—you awaken to the sights and sounds of a place different from home. Hopefully the bed was comfortable and your sleep was sound and restful. But that is already the past. On the road, once it has passed into the rearview mirror of life, it is just a memory stored for when the trip is done. Today is a new day and holds new adventures and memories yet to be made. For me, when I am road-tripping, I have a few primal concerns upon rising. First is a peek out through the curtains, which answers the first two high-order questions: Is the bike still there, and what is the weather like? If the bike is there, I know I am off to a good start. Weather dictates whether I remain on my travel plan or need to recalculate. These days, between the almost ubiquitous presence of cable television weather and Wi-Fi for my laptop, I can quickly reroute around weather, in most cases—although there have been times when all the information in the world wouldn't remove the overnight surprise of several inches of late spring snow, especially in the Great Lakes region. Those two questions answered, it is time to shower, dress, repack the bike, and move forward to the ultimate primal concern—breakfast!

So many chain motels now offer a free breakfast that I think many people just graze on the freebies and hit the road. I will admit to doing that on occasion, mostly when I am traveling to do shows and time is the most limited resource at hand. But show days, while incredibly fun and exciting, are nonetheless workdays first and foremost.

When I am traveling for the pure joy of traveling, I would much rather find a place that the locals frequent and leave the hotel freebies alone. At the counter of a diner or cafe

I can talk with the locals. Most folks find travelers interesting, especially motorcyclists, and are willing to talk. The locals might just know some great roads or a good place for finding lunch a few towns away. They can be a wealth of information or just good conversation. People are just as much a part of the fabric of the area you are traveling through as the roads and scenery. You might as well enjoy them. You never know who you might meet, perhaps a new friend.

An American diner and motorcycle, a perfect pair: Red Planet Diner, Sedona, Arizona, with Josh Placa's Harley-Davidson JOSHUA PLACA

Sometimes my choice of overnight accommodations is a bed-and-breakfast or a country inn, where the morning meal is as it should be, a celebration of the start of a new day. Sometimes sharing a table with fellow travelers is a real treat, much like things were in a bygone era when the world was simpler and there was always time to be social and make new acquaintances. In the time before television and the Internet, when motorized travel was still new and the roads still an ever-changing adventure, those opportunities to share knowledge and experience were very valuable to the traveler—especially if you were graced with the good fortune to share the morning meal with folks who were coming from where you were headed. Their sharing the most recent news on the conditions of the roads and what services and challenges lay ahead of you was the equivalent of our twenty-four-hour weather and news.

As time goes by, I find that I am more interested in the diverse experiences of traveling the roadscape of America than I am in just accumulating miles in the saddle. Each day's experiences can start by sharing the morning meal. Here are some breakfast treats to share at home, each from a place you might want to visit when you are on the road again.

White Grill, Nevada, Missouri

200 North Commercial Street
Nevada, MO 64772
(417) 667-9388

Lee Volmer of Odessa, Missouri, recommended the White Grill in Nevada, Missouri, telling me that his favorite dish there is called "The Mess." I reached out to the folks at the White Grill and spoke with Linda Gower, who told me the following:

"The small restaurant on the corner of Commercial and North Osage in Nevada, Missouri, has served presidents, famous ball players, and young couples on their dates. Harry S. Truman said, 'the best damn hamburger I ever ate.' Our hamburgers are made from fresh ground beef (never frozen), and our hash browns and Suzie Q's are done fresh as well. On our breakfast menu we are famous for our 'Mess'—a combination of hash browns, onions, choice of meat (ham, bacon, or sausage), egg, and cheese melted on top.

"The White Grill is the last one of the chain that was started by Harold 'Red' McLaughlin in 1938. In the 1950s Lawrence 'Frip' Wolfe and Bob Seaver purchased the drive-in from Red. Then, in 1964, James A. Novak bought into the business. In 1980 James and Shirley Novak bought out Frip and Bob. All of the original owners have passed away, but the business continues with the children and grandchildren of the Novaks.

"Bob Seaver remembered serving Gerald Ford's daughter, who sat up on the cigarette machine to take a picture of him. Since many of the Kansas City A's ball team came to the nearby Kelso Ranch to hunt and fish, they stopped by as well. Many travelers stop by as they travel through Nevada. We even have couples who met here come back and eat on their anniversary.

"We also have curb service—the last of its time; just honk, and we will come out and take your order. You talk to a person, not through a machine. We return with the order freshly cooked.

"We are still located in the same building. We have added on since 1938, and this summer we plan to add on again, so we will have eleven stools, two tables, and six booths.

"Remember, Harry S. Truman said, 'the best damn hamburger I ever ate.' We say the best damn hamburger in Nevada, Missouri."

The Mess

2 tablespoons oil or butter
4 cups diced potatoes
¼ cup chopped onions
1 cup chopped cooked ham (or precooked bacon or sausage)
2 medium eggs
4 slices American cheese (or your favorite cheese)

In a large frying pan, heat the oil or butter over high heat. Add the potatoes and onions and cook for 5 to 7 minutes or until lightly browned and tender, stirring often. Place the meat on top of the hash browns and stir in. Break the eggs over the mess and then stir in. Cook, stirring gently, until the eggs are done, about 2 to 3 minutes. When the eggs begin to firm, cover with the cheese, reduce the heat to medium, and cover. Continue cooking until the cheese is melted, about 2 minutes. Serve immediately.

Makes 1 large Mess or 2 regular servings.

Moose Café, Asheville, North Carolina

570 Brevard Road
Asheville, NC 28806
(828) 255-0920

The Moose Café has been an Asheville, North Carolina, landmark eatery for more than fifteen years. It is located right next to the Western North Carolina Farmers Market, giving the cafe great access to the freshest produce the mountains have to offer. Join them for breakfast, and you will be treated to a basket heaped full of light and fluffy biscuits and homemade apple butter. Western North Carolina is renowned for the locally grown apples, so you know the apple butter is tasty. Many local riders will start their Sunday rides with breakfast at the Moose, so you might find new riding buddies who can show you some of the best roads in western North Carolina. You can also try this tasty Hash Brown Casserole that has the flavor to stand alongside great biscuits and farm fresh eggs.

Hash Brown Casserole

1½ cups shredded potatoes
1 small onion, diced
½ cup crumbled bacon
1 can cream of chicken soup
1 cup chicken stock
½ cup sour cream
½ cup shredded cheddar cheese, plus
    extra for topping
1 teaspoon salt
½ teaspoon pepper

▪ **Preheat oven to 375°F.**

▪ **In a large mixing bowl, combine all ingredients. Mix together well and transfer to a well-greased casserole dish. Sprinkle additional cheese on top and bake uncovered for 45 minutes, or until the middle is firm.**

Makes 6–8 servings.

The Dillard House, Dillard, Georgia

1158 Franklin Street
Dillard, GA 30537
(706) 746-5348 or (800) 541-0671
www.dillardhouse.com

The Dillard House has a long and venerable history dating back to the last decade of the eighteenth century, when Capt. John Dillard received a one-thousand-acre land grant for his valiant service in the War for Independence. John Dillard, the great-great-great grandson of the captain, who, along with the Dillard family and friends, operates the Dillard House today, was kind enough to share some of his family recipes with me. If you are traveling in the South, you owe it to yourself to visit with the Dillard family. They have both a fine dining room and a quality range of accommodations to make your stay memorable.

I have selected three recipes that form a perfect Southern-style breakfast that is sure to fuel you well for a day's adventure exploring the old roads of northeastern Georgia. The recipes come from their wonderful cookbook, *The Dillard House Cookbook and Mountain Guide,* which John graciously shared with us. Try these recipes at home, and then make plans to visit our beloved Southern mountains. Let's start with my favorite baked treat: biscuits. To me, down-home Southern biscuits are better than any bread or cake could ever be.

Dillard House Buttermilk Biscuits

2½ cups plain flour
¼ teaspoon baking soda
½ teaspoon salt
2½ tablespoons baking powder
¾ cup shortening
1½ cups buttermilk

▨ **Preheat oven to 425°F.**

▨ **Sift together flour, baking soda, salt, and baking powder. Blend the shortening into the sifted flour mixture. Add buttermilk until well moistened, and mix thoroughly. Transfer dough to a floured surface and knead. Roll dough to ½-inch thickness. Cut biscuits with cutter. Place on greased baking sheet and bake for 10 to 12 minutes.**

Makes 2 dozen biscuits.

Back in 1916, Carrie Dillard opened her first boardinghouse, beginning what is now a three-generations-old tradition of treating guests like family. Whether in their all-you-can-eat dining room for breakfast, lunch, or dinner, or staying in the hotel or one of the chalets or cottages, you feel like you are back home visiting family.

Speaking of family-style breakfast, some folks will tell you that a biscuit without gravy is just plain not right. Believe them! So here is a red eye gravy that will wake up your taste buds.

- -

Dillard House Red Eye Gravy

4 large slices country ham
1 cup bacon drippings
1 tablespoon brown sugar
½ cup black coffee
½ cup water

■ **Fry ham in bacon drippings; remove ham and set aside. Add brown sugar, coffee, and water to drippings. Let come to a boil. Serve over grits, biscuits, or scrambled eggs. Gravy may be stored in the refrigerator and heated as needed.**

Makes 6–8 servings.

- -

To round out this threesome of great breakfast treats, I have chosen this casserole from *The Dillard House Cookbook and Mountain Guide.* It will give you a great grits experience, and, even if you are from way up north and haven't yet learned to love our traditional hot breakfast cereal, you will ask for more. You could add some side plates piled high with fresh eggs, melon, jams, and breakfast meats, and it would be close to being there—except that there is nothing like a mountain breakfast served with the Blue Ridge Mountains just outside of the front porch. You owe it to yourself to experience it, so motor on over, search out the old Dixie Highway or cruise the Blue Ridge Parkway, and, as that famous commercial said, "Just do it!"

Dillard House Grits and Sausage Casserole

1 cup uncooked grits
1 cup uncooked ground pork sausage
8 eggs, beaten
1½ cups milk
¼ teaspoon garlic salt
¼ teaspoon white pepper
3 tablespoons lightly salted butter or margarine
2 cups grated sharp cheddar cheese

▨ **Preheat oven to 350°F.**

▨ **Cook grits according to package directions. Set aside. Cook sausage over medium heat until browned, stirring to crumble. Drain on paper towels and set aside. Combine eggs, milk, garlic salt, and white pepper in a large bowl. Stir in cooked grits. Add butter and cheese, stirring until cheese melts. Stir in sausage. Pour mixture into a lightly greased 3-quart casserole dish. Bake uncovered for 1 hour or until set.**

Makes approximately 8 servings.

Mrs. Rowe's Restaurant and Bakery, Staunton, Virginia

74 Rowe Road
Staunton, VA 24401
(540) 886-1833
www.mrsrowes.com

Mrs. Rowe's Restaurant and Bakery is located on U.S. Highway 250, just east of Interstate 81 and the charming city of Staunton, Virginia. In this area of the country, US 250 is called the

Jefferson Highway, and Mrs. Rowe's is not too far from the junction of U.S. Highway 11, the Lee Highway, one of the main routes of my childhood travels. U.S. 250 is a spur highway of U.S. Highway 50, a major coast-to-coast highway; it connects with US 50 in Sandusky, Ohio, and starts in Richmond, Virginia. US 250 also connects with the juncture of the southern terminus of the Skyline Drive and the northern terminus of the Blue Ridge Parkway.

I am sure that as a child, with my mom, Aunt Devota, and Uncle Bunk, we ate at Mrs. Rowe's Restaurant. I am particularly pleased to have a few of her recipes in this book, courtesy of the new owner, Michael DiGrassie, and Mollie Bryan, who wrote a wonderful narrative cookbook called *Mrs. Rowe's Restaurant Cookbook: A Lifetime of Recipes from the Shenandoah Valley,* published by Ten Speed Press. Mollie told me, "This recipe was featured in *Southern Living* magazine as one of the South's most unique restaurant breakfasts." I am sure it will become one of your family favorites.

Mrs. Rowe's Pumpkin Pecan Pancakes

2 cups all-purpose flour
4 teaspoons baking powder
1 teaspoon ground cinnamon
½ teaspoon ground nutmeg
¼ teaspoon ground allspice
¾ cup sugar

1½ cups canned pumpkin
3 large eggs
1 cup milk
¾ cup vegetable oil
1 teaspoon vanilla extract
4 ounces chopped pecans

▦ Sift the flour, baking powder, cinnamon, nutmeg, allspice, and sugar into a large bowl.

▦ Stir the pumpkin, eggs, milk, oil, and vanilla together in another large bowl. Add the flour mixture to the pumpkin mixture and mix well. Fold in the pecans.

▦ Heat a greased griddle over medium-high heat. Use ¼ cup of batter for each pancake. Cook the pancakes on the first side until bubbles form in the center and they are browned on the bottom. Turn once and brown the other side. Serve hot with warm maple syrup.

Makes 4 servings.

3

Sandwiches and Lunch Specialties

A good midday meal is more important to a traveler than a lot of folks realize. I have some good friends who can make do with just a protein bar and a bottle of water at a gas stop and call that lunch. I also have friends who will eat a humongous meal replete with a rich dessert and then need a nap before riding on. Who wants to nap in the afternoon while touring anyway? That is prime riding and sightseeing time. Both of these extremes work for some folks, but many others and I prefer something different for the midday meal.

Here I have assembled a rather diverse collection of sandwiches and lunch specialties. Many of them would also do fine for a lighter dinner as well. One of them will even have you singing some Elvis tunes while you ride through the afternoon. (You know, the King was a Harley-Davidson rider.) However you take your lunchtime meal in, this is also a fine time to stretch your legs, and all of your muscles, for that matter. Whether you are riding a motorcycle, catching some breeze in a convertible, or piloting the family soccer-mom-mobile, your body needs to move around to get the circulation going and prevent stiffness. After a road lunch is a good time to get reinvigorated and restore your alertness before hitting the road again.

Of course, if you are making these recipes at home and don't have an afternoon's yard work to do, then swing out that hammock, pop some vintage Elvis vinyl on that dusty old turntable (okay, just click your iPod to the Elvis playlist), and, while you enjoy a siesta, dream of road-tripping across America.

Santa Fe Café & Lounge, Beavercreek, Ohio

3991 Dayton Xenia Road
Beavercreek, OH 45431
(937) 426-9222

Beavercreek, Ohio, is located southeast of Dayton along U.S. Highway 35. Farther east along US 35 you will find the town of Chillicothe, host to a famous stop on the Annual Easyrider Rodeo Tour. Continuing farther east on US 35, you will pass through Jackson, Ohio, where the road is designated the Bob Evans Highway until it reaches Gallipolis, Ohio, at the West Virginia state line and the Ohio River. There is a scenic bypass along the river on the Ohio side.

The Santa Fe Café & Lounge, a neighborhood biker bar located in Beavercreek, Ohio, is a place where everyone feels like they know each other, and owner Wanda Stewart has operated it for the last twenty years. They welcome motorcycle travelers, asking only that you respect their no-colors policy. When you visit them, try this sandwich and ask them how it got its name. One thing is sure: Wanda is right when she says, "careful, this is high cholesterol," but it packs enough protein to carry you to the state line.

- -

Santa Fe Café & Lounge's World Famous "Whiz Bang" Sandwich

1 large sesame bun
Mayonnaise
Lettuce
1 slice fried ham
1 fried egg

1 slice cheese (your choice)
2 or 3 pieces bacon
1 slice tomato
1 slice onion

Lightly toast the bun; spread mayonnaise on the bun bottom. Place the lettuce on the bun bottom, then the fried ham, fried egg, cheese, and bacon. Top with tomato and onion. Spread additional mayonnaise on the top half of the bun and close the sandwich. Serve immediately.

Makes 1 sandwich.

- -

The Old Salt, Hampton, New Hampshire

The Old Salt Eating & Drinking Place
490 Lafayette Road, Hampton, NH 03842
(603) 926-8322
www.oldsaltnh.com

My friends at Seacoast Harley-Davidson in North Hampton, New Hampshire, recommended the Old Salt restaurant to me. The folks at Seacoast HD are very fond of the Goody Cole Chicken Sandwich, and the Higgins family, who owns the Old Salt, were gracious enough to share the recipe with us. The Old Salt restaurant's original building was destroyed by fire in 1999. Two years later the Higgins family purchased the Lamie's Inn and reopened the locally beloved Old Salt. The Lamie's Inn structure has a long and storied history dating back to its construction as a home in 1740, which was then converted to a restaurant and tavern in 1928. Today it offers not just great food but also thirty-two colonial-style rooms in the inn, making it a perfect stop for travelers weary from a long day of exploring the historic roads and coast of New Hampshire.

      The recipe calls for a bulkie roll, which is a New England original type of fresh baked roll, but the folks at the Old Salt assure me you can substitute a Kaiser if you're not in New England.

- -

Goody Cole Chicken Sandwich

distilled water
2 cedar planks
1 (8-ounce) chicken breast
1 large bulkie roll
1 or 2 slices aged cheddar cheese
3 or 4 slices cooked bacon
Iceberg lettuce
Sliced ripe tomato
A few thin slices sweet red onion
Goody Cole Homemade Tarragon Mayo (optional;
     for the recipe, see the Travel Trailer chapter)

▨ Soak cedar planks in distilled water for 30 minutes. Fire up your grill. Place cedar planks directly over the flames or coals of your grill to create smoke.

▨ Remove skin and excess fat from the chicken breast. Proceed to charbroil your chicken breast by placing it directly on the grill above the smoking planks. Grill 7 minutes on one side, turn, and cook 5 minutes on the other side. The chicken is done when the juices that run out when a knife is poked through the breast are clear.

▨ When chicken is done, lightly toast your bulkie roll over the grill. If you prefer, spread the roll with Goody Cole Homemade Tarragon Mayo. Place the chicken on the bottom half of the roll. Top the chicken with cheese and bacon, and then cover with the top half of the roll. Serve with lettuce, tomato, and onion slices.

Makes 1 sandwich.

- -

Doyle's Pub & Eatery, Richmond, Illinois

Doyle's Pub & Eatery
5604 Mill Street, Richmond, IL 60071
(815) 678-3623
www.doylespubrocks.com

Let me share a little of the history of the building that houses Doyle's Pub as excerpted from their Web site:

"Doyle's Pub was first known as The Richmond Mill, which was originally built in 1844 by Charles Cotting & William Purdy. It is the second-oldest building in Richmond. The building was partially destroyed in a fire in 1925. The mill was turned into a restaurant in the 60s. It went through four owners from 1968 to 1994 and was vacant for many of those years.

"Jeanne Doyle opened Doyle's in November of 1994 and has owned and operated it ever since. Jeanne can be found in the kitchen most mornings making homemade soups, sauces, chili, salad dressing, and desserts. Oh, and don't forget about the fresh roasted corned beef for one of the finest Reubens around!

Bike Night at Doyle's Pub & Eatery DOYLE'S PUB & EATERY

"Doyle's is a family-friendly, rider-friendly, quaint Irish pub serving homemade foods and top-quality Irish beers such as Guinness, Smithwicks, and Harp, to name a few."

Jeanne tells me, "I have a couple of Milwaukee cops who come down here once a month for my Reuben! One secret is I use a round of corned beef, **not** a brisket. Another secret is my sauerkraut. This is an incredible sandwich—wash it down with a pint of Guinness or Carlsburg."

Did I mention they have the best Reuben around? The recipe makes seven to eight sandwiches depending on how high you pile the meat and how much your beef cooks down (the five-pound round will cook down to about three and a half pounds). You will have enough sauerkraut to make the sandwiches and some left over to serve on the side for all those "kraut lovers."

- -

Jeanne's Best Reuben Anywhere

The Meat
1 (5-pound) round of corned beef
½ cup pickling spice

▧ **Preheat oven to 400°F.**

▧ **Cover the beef round in pickling spice and place in roasting pan. Fill the pan half full of water and place on stovetop over a high heat. Bring to a boil, boil for 20 minutes, and then remove pan from the heat. Carefully cover the pan with foil and bake in oven for 2 hours.**

▧ **Cool the beef completely, then slice thin for sandwiches.**

The Sauerkraut
1 (1-pound) can of sauerkraut
⅛ cup brown sugar
¼ cup applesauce
¼ teaspoon ground fennel seed
¼ cup Guinness beer (but any good beer will do)

▧ **In medium saucepan over a low heat, combine the sauerkraut, brown sugar, applesauce, fennel seed, and beer. Slowly simmer for 2 hours, stirring occasionally.**

Jeanne's Best Reuben Anywhere   DOYLE'S PUB & EATERY

The Reuben Assembly
Dark rye bread
Butter
Thousand Island dressing
Swiss cheese

Take two pieces of dark rye bread and butter one side of each; these will be on the outside of the sandwich. Lay the two pieces of bread butter side down on a piece of waxed paper, and spread thousand island dressing on both pieces of bread (this is the inside of the sandwich). Lay a slice of Swiss cheese over the dressing on both slices of bread. Place a scoop of sauerkraut on one piece of bread and pile the corned beef as high as you wanna go on the other piece of bread. Close the sandwich and transfer to a hot flat-top grill or a frying pan (not too hot of a pan or the bread will burn). Fry for 3 to 4 minutes over medium heat, and then turn over and fry on the other side for 3 to 4 minutes or until the cheese melts. Serve piping hot.

Makes 7–8 Reuben sandwiches.

Arnold's Drive-In, Decatur, Indiana

222 North Thirteenth Street
Decatur, IN 46733
(260) 728-4740

Harley-Davidson rider Chuck Johnson, who lives in northeastern Indiana about 35 miles north of Fort Wayne, says, "Arnold's Drive-In in Decatur, Indiana, is a place you won't soon forget. Arnold's is a 1950s/60s-style drive-in complete with all the necessary decor, right down to the neon lights and car hops on roller skates. Their menu has all the favorites—burgers, fries, and tenderloins that can be completed with an old-fashioned-style malt, shake, or even a phosphate. My favorite is their tenderloin and onion rings. On the weekend, Arnold's is the place to be to check out some vintage rides at the Cruise-In."

Lori Collier is the third generation of family owner-operators at Arnold's; it had originally been called the Penguin Point Restaurant when her grandparents opened it. Lori shared a few recipes from her must-visit drive-in, saying about this one, "Here is the recipe for 'the King's' favorite sandwich—I tweaked it just a little to give it, I think, an even better taste—'Elvis's Deep-Fried Peanut Butter and Banana Sandwich.' Now ya got a sandwich fit for a king! 'Thank you, thank you very much!'"

She went on to say, "Elvis made this a little different: He mashed the banana and mixed it with the peanut butter and simply put it on toasted bread. I'm sure he liked it that way, Billy, but without a doubt, he would be 'all shook up' over my version. Whenever we make this for a customer, we sound off this police siren we have in the dining room, and the servers all yell, 'Elvis has left the kitchen!' Hope you like this recipe."

Elvis's Deep-Fried Peanut Butter and Banana Sandwich

3 tablespoons creamy peanut butter
2 slices cinnamon raisin bread
½ banana, sliced into 3 long strips
2 cups Drake's brand batter mix
Powdered sugar

■ Preheat a deep fryer to 365°F. The oil level should be deep enough to submerge a sandwich without overflowing.

■ Spread peanut butter on both slices of bread. Place the banana strips on one of the slices of bread. Put the other slice of bread on top to make a sandwich. Mix the Drake's mix with water and stir to make a thick "pancakelike" consistency. Completely submerge the sandwich into the mix, making sure to coat every inch of bread, including the creases!

■ Immediately submerge into deep fryer. It is best to put the sandwich in something like a fryer basket, and then I put another basket directly on top so it will be totally sunk in oil. Turn over after about 1 minute and again submerge. Be careful not to let the basket stick to the wet dip mix. It will be done after 3 to 3½ minutes of deep frying. Let cool 1 minute, cut diagonally, and finish by dusting with powdered sugar.

Makes 1 sandwich.

Top of the Hill Grill, Brattleboro, Vermont

632 Putney Road
Brattleboro, VT 05301
(802) 258-9178
www.topofthehillgrill.com

This fabulous barbecue joint was recommended by my friend Sue Carney and her team at the American Postal Workers Union (APWU), whom I have had the honor of working with to support our wounded veterans. Here is what she had to say:

"It was a weekend to be remembered. Our union members had a blast riding with you in Rolling Thunder XX. And I am sure we created many fond memories for the wounded troops during the barbecue APWU hosted for them at the Mologne House in Washington, D.C.

"As the National Human Relations Director for the American Postal Workers Union, I would not consider myself a roadhouse expert by any stretch of the imagination (most of my travel is by plane), but thanks to the kindhearted hospitality of APWU members from across the country I have been blessed with hundreds of dining excursions. I thought you might enjoy sharing some of our favorite spots. Beth Edwards, APWU secretary and former Brattleboro resident, recommended the Top of the Hill Grill.

"This is an absolutely *great* barbecue joint—terrific food and a fantastic view from the outside deck. They also have indoor seating with a coal stove for when it's a little chilly. A personal favorite is the pulled pork roll-up on a jalapeño tortilla. Ask for extra sauce! They keep hot sauce at the window, so the heat lovers among us can raise the bar a notch or two if so inclined. The beef brisket and the chili are also excellent. The owner, Jon, is a very friendly guy who can often be found at the smoker. He loves to talk barbecue or just about anything else."

Sue and Beth were right: I spent a good while on the phone with Jon, and he is very enthusiastic about his food and hospitality. I feel like I have a new friend in Vermont now. Along with this recipe here, in Jon Julian's own words, is what he had to say:

"This roll-up is a true original. The Brattleboro, Vermont, area is known for its 'alternative'-type lifestyle. There are a sizeable number of vegetarians here, and though I run a barbecue joint, I did not want to exclude the non–meat eaters in our midst. I was looking for a vegetarian barbecue experience that wasn't trying to fake being a hamburger. This is simple, nutritious, and satisfying in a hearty kind of way. The add-ons allow for lots of variations."

Biker Billy rides with the American Postal Workers Union in the Rolling Thunder XX Parade. SUE CARNEY, APWU

- -

Top of the Hill Grill Tempeh Roll Up

3 tablespoons toasted sesame oil
8 ounces plain tempeh cakes, cubed (we use the Lite Life brand found in the health food
    section of the grocery)
1 small green pepper, sliced into thin strips
1 small sweet onion, sliced into thin strips (we use Vidalia onions when in season)
Splash of a good quality soy sauce (we use Kikkoman)
1 (10-inch) tortilla (we use flavored, i.e. garlic/herb,jalapeño/cheddar, etc.)
Barbecue sauce to taste (we use traditional tomato-based sauce with a moderate kick and a
    smoky top note)

Optional Add-Ons
Shredded cheese (we use a cheddar and Monterey Jack blend)
Coleslaw
Salad greens
Rice
Black beans

Heat the oil in a medium sauté pan over a medium/high heat until hot but not smoking. (Sesame oil has a low smoke point, so be careful not to burn it.) Add the tempeh, peppers, and onion, and stir-fry for 2 to 3 minutes, or until the onions soften a little. Add splash of soy sauce; it can be salty, so go lightly.

In another preheated pan (a large flat skillet works best), lightly toast the tortilla. Thirty seconds per side should be enough.

Carefully remove the tortilla and lay on a flat surface. Spoon the tempeh sauté onto the tortilla. Top with barbecue sauce and/or your favorite toppings.

Roll into a log, remembering to tuck in the sides.

Makes 1 serving.

Jo Jo's Pizza & Soft Ice Cream, Ancram, New York

1015 Route 82
Ancram, NY 12502
(518) 851-6567

Susan Buck, a longtime moto-journalist and a good friend of mine, shared this restaurant and got Carlo to share his secret Stromboli recipe. In Susan's words:

"**Lunch break: I live in New York City, where no matter how you like pizza, it's better than anywhere else. I've sampled slices near and far, but the only place for true satisfaction is within the five boroughs. I run up the Taconic Parkway at least a few times a year, and while the tank is rarely close to empty, I always stop at Jo Jo's pizzeria.**

"**Discovering pizza worth stopping for one hundred miles north of the Whitestone Bridge had me infatuated, but after the spinach Stromboli I was completely seduced. The pastry is thin and crisp. The spinach is brilliant green and flavorful, not overcooked. The cheese is creamy and chunky, not gooey and gummy. Some chunky, fresh-tasting marinara sauce for dipping? Yes, please.**"

Take a ride up the famous Taconic Parkway, which was originally built in the late 1920s and early 1930s as a scenic drive from New York City to the Bear Mountain Bridge. You will find more traffic these days, but it is still restricted to passenger vehicles only, making it more enjoyable on a motorcycle.

- -

Carlo's Spinach Stromboli

3 tablespoons extra virgin olive oil,
　plus extra
3 (1-pound) packages thawed frozen
　spinach
4 cloves finely chopped garlic
1 cup ricotta cheese

1 (½ pounds) pizza dough
1 cup shredded mozzarella cheese
Sesame seeds

▓ Preheat oven to 400°F. Grease a large baking pan with (the extra) olive oil.

▓ Cook the spinach in a large pot of boiling water over medium heat for 5 minutes, and then drain thoroughly.

▓ While spinach is cooking, heat the olive oil in a small sauté pan over medium heat, add the garlic, and sauté for 5 minutes, or until tender; do not allow to brown.

▓ In a large mixing bowl, combine the spinach with the sautéed garlic and olive oil, toss well, and allow to cool to room temperature.

▓ Lightly fold in the ricotta cheese. Do not over mix—you want to have clumps of cheese and clumps of spinach.

▓ On a floured board with a floured roller, roll out the pizza dough into a long, stretched-out oval about 24 inches long by 6 inches wide. Sprinkle the mozzarella cheese onto the center of the dough, leaving about 1 inch uncovered around the edge. Scoop the spinach mixture onto the center of the cheese-covered dough. Pull the sides up so that they cover the filling and overlap each other, and then fold over the ends like you would when making a burrito. Place the overlapped side on the bottom in the greased pan. Cut slits into the top of the Stromboli, sprinkle with some oil and sesame seeds, and bake until golden brown, about 15 minutes.

Makes 1 Stromboli.

- -

The Time Warp Tea Room, Knoxville, Tennessee

1209 North Central Street
Knoxville, TN 37917
(865) 524-1155
www.timewarpvmc.org

The Time Warp Tea Room is a favorite local place to visit for Knoxville, Tennessee, area riders; they host events from "Bike Nights" to "Swap Meets" here. Here's a blurb from their Web site:

"The Time Warp Tea Room, at 1209 North Central in Knoxville, Tennessee, is owned by Daniel P. Moriarty. He opened the tearoom and coffee shop in October 2002, after using the building for many years to store coin-operated machines that he maintains for area businesses. The Tea Room is a place like no other in the world, offering a selection of beverages and foods in a decor of antiques and motorcycle memorabilia. Where else can one play a forty-year-old pinball machine amid walls covered with 1980s *Cycle News?*"

The Grilled Club is the Time Warp Tea Room's best-selling sandwich; try it at home, and the next time you come to the Honda Hoot, warp on over and visit them.

Grilled Club Sandwich

2 slices bread (honey wheat, Texas toast, or rye)
Time Warp Seasoned Grilling Oil (for the recipe, see the Travel Trailer chapter)
4 ounces black forest ham
4 ounces smoked turkey breast
3 ounces crisp bacon
1 slice cheddar cheese
Handful mixed baby greens (arugula, red leaf, romaine, radicchio, green leaf, and mustard)
Sliced tomatoes
Mayonnaise
Pickle slices
Sliced pickled banana peppers
Potato chips

▓ Preheat contact grill (such as a George Foreman or a sandwich press).

▓ Brush each slice of bread on one side with Time Warp Seasoned Grilling Oil. Layer on ham, turkey, bacon, and cheese. Grill until golden brown. Remove from grill, open sandwich, and add baby greens, tomatoes, and mayonnaise. Serve with pickles, banana peppers, and potato chips.

Makes 1 sandwich.

Stoney Knob Cafe, Weaverville, North Carolina

337 Merrimon Avenue
Weaverville, NC 28787
(828) 645-3309
www.stoneyknobcafe.com

This recipe comes from one of my local favorite places. Mary and I both enjoy them so much that we took our wedding rehearsal dinner there. When we go there for Sunday breakfast, we will arrive at least 15 minutes before they open so we can get a table—they are so popular that the parking lot is almost always completely filled.

Here is what they say on their Web site:

Chef Yotty Dermas of the Stoney Knob Café with some of his creations ANTHONY MARTIN

"'Hip, funky and exotic' are just a few of the ways diners describe Stoney Knob Café. This unique restaurant offers its guests cuisine from near and far, with an eclectic menu including American contemporary, Greek and European dishes, gourmet pizzas, fantastic hors d'oeuvres and a variety of Southern comfort foods.

Stoney Knob has the hippest outdoor patio scene going on, with live music in the spring and summer. In the fall and winter you can cozy up by the fire in the warm and sexy Red Room and enjoy a lovely non-smoking atmosphere over a really great bottle of wine from their extensive wine list. It's the perfect place for your own private party, whether it's dinner for two or a dozen.

Family owned and operated for over 40 years, Stoney Knob Café is located in Weaverville just off the New Stock Road exit on I-26 West/19-23 North, only 10 minutes from Asheville. Reservations suggested but not required."

I would suggest a reservation by all means, especially during peak season at traditional mealtimes. Even if you have to wait it is well worth it.

Black Bean Hummus Wrap

2 cups cooked black beans
Pinch of salt
Pinch of cayenne
Pinch of fresh black peppercorn
1 tablespoon lemon juice
1 tablespoon paprika
1 teaspoon honey
1 teaspoon cumin
1 teaspoon coriander
1 tablespoon tahini paste

2 ounces olive oil
2 (10-inch) tortillas
½ cup feta cheese, crumbled
4 ounces blanched broccoli, cut into
    bite-size pieces
1 roasted portobello mushroom, cut
    into bite-size pieces
1 roasted red pepper, cored and
    julienned

In a food processor equipped with a chopping blade combine the black beans, salt, cayenne, black peppercorn, lemon juice, paprika, honey, cumin, coriander, tahini, and olive oil; process until well combined and creamy, 20 seconds or so.

To assemble, steam the tortillas, then spread on the hummus mixture, then add the feta cheese, broccoli, mushrooms, and roasted red pepper. Roll to a burrito shape then slice in the middle.

Makes 2 servings.

4

Burgers and Dogs

I think if you say "road food," there are two things that pop into people's minds immediately: burgers and dogs. Whether it is a fast-food drive-through or a roadside truck or a street-corner pushcart, the mantra is Burgers and Dogs. As American as the flag, apple pie, and Mom—burgers and dogs—you get the idea. Could you disagree? I just don't think so. But you might be surprised from whence these tasty morsels of protein have their ancestry.

The humble hamburger has many claimants to the title of inventor, most dating from the 1880s. But the identity of the genius of the grill who first placed a cooked patty of beef between two pieces of bread and served it really doesn't matter very much at all. It was already an American tradition before the first motorcycle crossed the continent. As the earliest mentions of a ground beef steak were to call it a "Hamburg Steak," due to the origins of that recipe in Germany, and Hamburg being the largest embarkation port for immigrants coming to the United States, there was at the time a loose association between Germans and hamburgers. By the time of World War I, hamburgers were so common and the Germans so unpopular that the term "Salisbury steak" was coined to describe the ground beef steak. The hamburger sandwich was unpopular even after the war, until a company called White Castle introduced their trademarked Slyders, small square burgers "sold by the sack," and brought the concept back into the hearts of the American public.

The humble hot dog can top the hamburger when it comes to claims of who, where, and when it was invented. Claims go back as far as the 1480s, in Frankfurt, Germany, with a sausage, hence the name "frankfurter." Some place a German immigrant named Charles

Beau Allen Pacheco enjoys a Storm's hamburger. BEAU ALLEN PACHECO

Feltman at Coney Island, New York, selling sausages in rolls in 1870. Like its burger brother, it doesn't matter who did it first or where. Whether you call them franks, dogs, wieners, or tube steaks, they are vastly popular. A method of serving them called "Coney Dogs" appears to have no connection with Coney Island, but rather is a Midwest style. Many places that serve them guard their secret "Coney Sauce" like gold in Fort Knox, but fear not, in this chapter is a recipe from a wonderful place that shared their secret sauce. Well, okay, it isn't the exact recipe for their secret sauce. If we gave it out, it wouldn't be secret anymore now would it? However, they have provided a similar recipe for the sauce that is very, very good. But if you do want the real thing, you'll have to start planning a ride. I guarantee it will be worth the trip.

So whether your road hunger calls for a burger or screams cheeseburger or bellows gourmet burger; if your belly is barking for a hot dog with onion sauce or howling for a full-on Coney Dog, I've got you covered. So run, don't walk to the kitchen and get cooking with these recipes. Then grab some napkins and maps and sit down and enjoy. While you eat, you can plan your route to the homes of these road food legends.

Jersey Dogs Mobile, Roselle, New Jersey

Jersey Dogs Mobile
Warnaco Park, New Jersey Highway 27
Roselle, New Jersey

For the past five years, the Jersey Dogs Mobile truck has been a welcome sight and recharging repast for travelers along New Jersey Highway 27 in Roselle, New Jersey. Owner-operator Jim Shaw has been riding motorcycles for more than twenty-five years and currently rides a 2003 Road King Classic. One of the items that the truck and Jim are famous for is his Hot Onions Sauce recipe—it has been known to warm riders' palates and keeps them coming back for more. The truck is a 1983 AM General Postal Truck that Jim converted to the Jersey Dogs Mobile. Every year Rolling Thunder has its annual run for POWs and MIAs of the Vietnam War starting in Warnaco Park, New Jersey, in September. From the park, the run goes down NJ 27 to the Garden State Parkway and south to the POW/MIA memorial in Homedale, New Jersey. If you are traveling through northern New Jersey, take a run along NJ 27 in Roselle; you will find Jim and the Jersey Dogs Mobile outside of Warnaco County Park. Just remember to bring your appetite.

Jim Shaw and the Jersey Dogs Mobile JIM SHAW

Jim's Famous Jersey Dogs Hot Onions Sauce

1½ teaspoons olive oil
1 medium onion, sliced thin and chopped
4 cups water
2 tablespoons tomato paste
2 teaspoons corn syrup
1 teaspoon cornstarch
½ teaspoon salt
¼ teaspoon crushed red pepper flakes
¼ cup vinegar
1 habañero pepper, diced

Heat the oil in a large saucepan over medium heat.

Sauté onion in the oil for 5 minutes, or until the onion is soft, but not brown.

Add the water, tomato paste, corn syrup, cornstarch, salt, and red pepper flakes, and stir together.

Bring the mixture to a boil, and then reduce heat to low and simmer for 45 minutes.

Add the vinegar and habanero and continue simmering for an additional 30–45 minutes, or until most of the liquid is reduced and the sauce is thickened.

Makes about 2 cups.

View from The Haunted Hamburger JOSHUA PLACA

The Haunted Hamburger, Jerome, Arizona

410 North Clark Street
Jerome, AZ 86331
(520) 634-0554

My longtime friend and moto-journalist colleague Josh Placa recommended the Haunted Hamburger in Jerome, Arizona to me; here is what he had to say about it.

"There does dwell within these creaky walls and creepy spaces, souls restless and playful and apparently, in the strange case of the Haunted Hamburger, still dying of hunger. Consider the poor lonely spirit who can smell the irresistible aroma of roasting meat but cannot taste a single savory bite. The old copper boomtown of Jerome hosts a couple of century-old saloons, at least a dozen dearly departed bordellos, and an unspeakable number of life-challenged entities, many of whom would like nothing better to sit down to one last hot fleshy meal at this tasty eatery."

Josh Placa's Harley-Davidson parked outside The Haunted Hamburger, Jerome, Arizona JOSHUA PLACA

Brett Jurisin from the Haunted Hamburger was gracious enough to share this recipe with us and told me this about their fine eatery.

"The Haunted Hamburger is located on the side of Mingus Mountain in Jerome, Arizona, elevation 5,200 feet. Looking out from the restaurant over the Verde Valley you can see for over 70 miles on clear day, including Sedona and Humphreys Peak. Originally an old boardinghouse for the miners in Jerome, the building became a restaurant in the early 1970s.

It went through many owners until 1993, when it opened as the Haunted Hamburger, and it has become a very popular for stop for bikers and visitors of all types in Jerome. The restaurant serves burgers, cheesesteaks, chicken sandwiches, fajitas, steaks, and its award-winning barbecue baby back ribs. Drink specialties are margaritas and cold beer."

The Haunted Burger

½ pound patty ground beef
Fresh baked Kaiser roll
1 oz slice Swiss cheese
1 oz slice cheddar cheese
2 strips bacon
1 oz grilled onions
1 oz grilled mushrooms
1 oz grilled diced green chilies
2 oz guacamole

Fire up your grill.

Grill the ground beef patty on both sides to the desired level of doneness.

Lay the Kaiser roll open on a plate, and place one slice of cheese on the bottom half of the roll. Place the cooked burger on the cheese and cover with the other slice of cheese. Then layer with the bacon, onions, mushrooms, and green chilies. Spread the guacamole on the top half of the roll, close, and enjoy!

Makes 1 burger.

Squeeze Inn, Sacramento, California

7916 Fruitridge Road
Sacramento, CA 95820
(916) 386-8599
www.thesqueezeinn.com

Bob Parks from California recommended the Squeeze Inn in Sacramento, saying, "Ya got to eat at the Squeeze Inn in Sacramento. If this isn't the best cheeseburger on the planet, well, I can't believe it isn't. Too bad it is not a secret anymore, but it is still the best. I do cheeseburgers and ribs wherever I travel, and there is no equal to this cheeseburger."

Owner and chef Travis Hausauer shared his famous Squeeze Burger recipe and offers the following advice for all the home cooks out there.

"To make three burgers, start out with 1 pound of 80/20 ground beef (you can substitute leaner ground beef but will sacrifice taste). One of the most important parts is the bun. You need a good sourdough bun, not a hard roll. We use mild cheddar cheese; you can substitute your favorite cheese. Our Web site shows what the burgers look like when we cook them, and you can stay posted on the opening of our second location."

Here is an except from the Squeeze Inn Web site:

"Welcome to the **SQUEEZE INN!** If you're looking for the best burgers in town, then you've come to the right place. Located near the corner of Fruitridge and Power Inn in lower Sacramento, this Best of Sacramento multiple award winner is the perfect place to go if you're looking for a great place to fill your belly. Come check us out."

There you have it, folks, so try these burgers at home, and if you are in Sacramento, California, squeeze on over and pay them a visit.

Squeeze Burger

1 pound 80/20 ground beef
Lawry's Seasoned Salt
3 sourdough buns
¾ pound shredded mild cheddar cheese (you can substitute your favorite cheese)
Long sliced dill pickles
Red and yellow onion slices
Tomato slices
Lettuce
Mustard
Mayonnaise

Pat out three burgers as equal in size/weight as possible. Season to taste with the Lawry's seasoning salt.

Heat a large cast-iron frying pan over medium heat and place the burgers in with about 3 inches separating them. Cook the burgers until they reach an internal temperature of 157°F. Flip the burgers and put a handful of cheese (about a quarter of a pound) on top of each one. The cheese will overflow the top of the burgers onto the pan surrounding the burgers; you want this to happen.

Place a bun top on the cheese that covers each burger, and then put some small pieces of ice around the cheese. This generates steam and, in turn, softens the bun and melts the cheese all around the burger.

While you wait for the cheese to melt, you can make up the bottom buns to your liking with the pickles, onions, tomatoes, lettuce, mustard, and mayonnaise. Once the cheese is melted and turns a light brown on the bottom, remove the burgers from the pan and place on your bottom buns—make sure you get all the overflowed cheese. Let cool for a few moments and enjoy.

Makes 3 Squeeze Burgers.

The Red Planet Diner, Sedona, Arizona

1655 W Highway 89A
Sedona, AZ 86336
(928) 282-6070

Josh Placa recommended this Turkey Burger from one of his favorite places in Sedona, Arizona. Josh is a writer, rider and wanderer, and a man with an appetite. Here is what he told me regarding this burger.

"The unearthly Red Planet Diner wears a celestial motif complete with miniature spaceships and various aliens hanging from the walls and ceilings of this Sedona, Arizona eatery; a hauntingly beautiful place of towering red rocks just a short teleportation from Area 51. Sedona is a timeless, sometimes surreal motorcycling mecca filled with spiritual vortices, the remains of ancient inland seas and thankfully, at least one joint where a ravenous biker can dematerialize a juicy turkey burger and a piquant solar salad."

Turkey Burger

1 (7-ounce) all-white meat turkey patty
Burger bun or roll
Tomato slices
Onion slices (grilled preferred)

Lettuce
Mayonnaise (optional)
Ketchup (optional)
Mustard (optional)

▨ **Fire up your grill.**

▨ **Place the turkey patty on the grill and cook for approximate 6 minutes, flip and cook on the other side for an additional 6 minutes. Place the burger on the bottom half of the bun and add tomato, onion, and lettuce. Dress with your choice of optional condiments.**

Makes 1 serving.

Arnold's Drive-In, Decatur, Indiana

222 North Thirteenth Street
Decatur, IN 46733
(260) 728-4740

What is a classic Coney dog without sauce? Naked, that's what. Well, here is a slight variation on Lori Collier's famous (secret) 57 Classic Coney Sauce to ensure your dog will be sharply dressed. As Lori told me:

"Hey Biker Billy, here is my famous '57 Classic Coney Sauce' recipe (you will need a 10 gallon kettle for this). I use my own homemade utensil to stir this one. I use my Makita drill with a paint mixing attachment on the end to blend it all together. I should really get in touch with the Home Depot to get this one on the market; but do whatever works best for you. Personally, I like the feeling of power I get when I have the Makita in my hands!"

Can't think of what to do with 10 gallons of sauce? Well, if you sat and watched at Arnold's Drive-In, you would know just how fast that sauce goes. But while it might not go *as* fast at your house, there's no reason to cut down the recipe. Make it all. And then freeze it. When you thaw out your leftoevers, they will be as good as fresh, and you'll be very happy to have them ready to eat and at your fingertips.

57 Classic Coney Sauce

water (this should be the total of the first amount in the pot and for the flour mixture)
5 pounds white onions, diced
Handful of salt
3 pounds dark chili powder
5 heaping tablespoons cumin
1 level teaspoon cayenne pepper
2 teaspoons red pepper seasoning
1 tablespoon black pepper
1 cup Worcestershire sauce
20 pounds hamburger meat (the fattier, the better)
2 (96-ounce) cans ketchup puree
1 (96-ounce) can ketchup
Flour

Put 4 gallons of water in a large pot and add the onions, and salt. Place over a high heat and bring to a full boil. Add the chili powder, cumin, cayenne pepper, red pepper, black pepper seasoning, and Worcestershire sauce. Stir this all together and turn down the temperature a notch.

Break up the hamburger meat and put in the pot along with the puree and ketchup; blend it all together. Cook for 20 to 30 minutes at medium heat or until the sauce is smooth.

While the sauce is cooking, combine the flour and water in a large bowl and blend well. Add this to the sauce and blend in well. Continue to cook the sauce for another 5 minutes or until the sauce thickens.

Serve warm on the dogs.

Makes 10 gallons of sauce.

Arnold's 57 Classic Coney Dogs

Knowing how they make the "57 Classic Coney Sauce" at Arnold's is only part of the story in re-creating one of their famous 57 Classic Coney Dogs. So that you can have the whole experience at home (well, as close as it comes outside of Decatur, Indiana, that is), I asked Lori how they do it at the drive-in. She told me:

"We make our '57 Classic Coney' by first putting the Coney sauce on, then add one fine line of yellow mustard, and then top it off with diced white onions. It doesn't get any better than that, people! Our Coney dog recipe started over seventy-five years ago in my grandma's kitchen and lives on today. Our Coney dogs are so good, they will make your tongue beat your brain to death! Thanks, Grandma!"

There you have it. All the details are below for you to follow step by step.

6 hot dogs
6 toasted hot dog buns
57 Classic Coney Sauce

Yellow mustard
1 cup diced white onions

▨ **Boil the hot dogs.**

▨ **Place a dog on a toasted bun and spoon on a generous amount of the 57 Classic Coney Sauce. Add one fine line of yellow mustard, and then top it off with the onions. Enjoy!**

Makes 6 Coney dogs.

Storm's Drive-In, Hamilton, Texas

923 East Main (Highway 36)
Hamilton, TX 76531
(254) 386-3143
www.stormsrestaurants.com
Also in Lampasas, Burnet, Marble Falls, and Kingsland, Texas

My longtime friend, fellow moto-journalist, and raconteur par excellence Beau Allen Pacheco recently relocated to Texas, from where he shared this recommendation with me.

"You never know when you'll find them, those hamburgers that reaffirm your faith in life on the planet. Those pre-diet, pre–cholesterol-counting, pre–fat-gram-counting, pre-Atkins, pre–Weight Watchers mounds of transcendental taste that restore your harmony in the first bite. They might be in the big city, or small town, in a shopping center, or the tragic megaplex. But when they're a surprise, it's because you were wise enough to eschew franchises and took a chance on a mom-and-pop place on your route. Such a place is Storm's in Hamilton, Texas. Burgers deluxe—burgers *a mundo*—burgers to ride a thousand miles for. Burgers whose memory will haunt you for weeks, beckoning you back like the sirens of Odysseus. Tall burgers with layers of meat in mind-bending configurations. Consider the Cordon Bleu Burger."

Well, with a recommendation like that, I had to know more about this place called Storm's Drive-In, so here is the lowdown from Robbis Storm:

"The original Storm's Drive-In in Lampasas is certainly venerable. There are not many restaurants that have been in the same family for almost sixty years. I was five years old when I 'helped' my dad build it back in 1950. He died in 1985, but my mom is still alive (ninety-seven), and up until 2007, was still active in the restaurant. During the late 1950s one of our regular customers was Elvis Presley, who was stationed at Fort Hood, some 30 miles away. Some people find it interesting that I personally waited on Elvis. I was thirteen or fourteen years old, and I think the year was 1959. When I realized who it was, I got tongue-tied. I couldn't think of a thing to say, so I just told him what the price was and took his money. As I recall he ordered a strawberry malt and tipped me a quarter, which was a handsome sum back then. My mom waited on him a number of times and said he was always very polite. He

Storm's Drive-In, Hamilton, Texas BEAU ALLEN PACHECO

did like our cheeseburgers. That was a long time ago, and my memory sometimes slips, but it seems like he ordered them with bacon on them.

"One of the things that make a Storm's hamburger different from other burgers is the fact that we still process our own meat, just like Dad did back in the 1950s. We cook each burger by hand, the traditional way. Our french fries are also done the old-fashioned way in that the spuds are always fresh, never frozen, and we still slice them by hand every day. I am proud to say we were one of the first drive-ins I know of to quit using trans fat in our fryers.

"We now have a presence in five Hill Country towns: Lampasas, Hamilton, Burnet, Marble Falls, and Kingsland. But we're not a chain. Of course, each location uses the same fine beef in its burgers, but each store is different. For example, Burnet and Kingsland Storm's both feature hand-breaded catfish and chicken-fried steak. Kingsland Storm's is unique in that it's on Lake LBJ, where you can tie up your boat and order from the dock. Each Storm's welcomes bikers."

Cordon Bleu Burger

2 pounds quality ground beef, divided
      into 8 patties
4 large hamburger buns
Mayonnaise or salad dressing
8 tomato slices

Sliced lettuce
Salt
8 thin slices cooked ham
4 slices American cheese

■ Preheat griddle or skillet to 350°F.

■ Cook the patties either on a griddle or in a very hot skillet. This is a four-step process. First, sear patties on one side so that they have a glaze, that is, until they're slightly caramelized. How long you cook the patties depends on two variables: (1) how done you want the meat and (2) how hot your griddle or skillet is. On our griddle we cook about 3 minutes for "just" done.

■ Let me clarify the procedure. Step one: Put the raw meat on the griddle (griddle should be brought to cooking temperature of 350°F before you put the meat on). Step two: Within 30 seconds, turn the meat over and mash it flatter so it sticks to your cooking surface. Step three: Let the meat cook for 2 or 3 minutes to acquire the glaze.

■ While you're cooking the meat, grill or toast the buns so that the two inner sides are golden brown. Then apply mayonnaise, two slices of tomatoes, and lettuce to the bottom bun.

■ Step four: Turn patty a second time. When the meat is done, salt lightly to taste, and begin layering in this order: One beef patty, one slice ham, one slice cheese, one slice ham, and top off with one more beef patty. Finally, put the upper bun on top of what now is a stack of beef, ham, and cheese. Place the stack on top of the dressed lower bun. Serve with french fries or onion rings.

Makes 4 burgers.

5

Soups

If you travel by road, especially on a motorcycle, sooner or later you will get rained on. The frequency and severity of rain seems to be in direct proportion to a few things. First on the order of magnitude is when and how well you washed your motorcycle. It is a known fact that if you wash your motorcycle before a long trip, it will rain. Wash and wax it to better-than-showroom perfection and travel to a rally, and the whole week will be wet.

Next up the ladder is rain gear. Go ahead and save a few bucks and buy that discounted rain gear in that el cheapo mail order catalog. After all, it is bright yellow, so not only will it keep you dry, it will enhance your visibility. Fat chance on staying dry in that junk; the wind at highway speed will shred that faster than a food processor shreds cheddar cheese. But you will be visible, since you will have large yellow streamers waving from your arms, legs, and middle. Okay, so you say you are a pro: You got the best rain gear money can buy; you could stand in a hotel shower until the town water tower runs dry and not get wet inside that super rain suit. Just make sure that you pack it. If you leave it at home, as soon as you are just far enough away that you wouldn't want to go back for it, the first raindrops will fall. And even if the forecast is for drought conditions, don't pack it on the bottom of your bag. A rain suit packed on the bottom of a saddlebag is a surefire deterrent to suiting up under overpasses or any other form of shelter. You will be soaked, and so will all your gear on top of the rain suit by the time you dig it out. (By the way, that is usually when the rain stops and you see that triple rainbow.)

If you are thinking of tempting fate and plan to leave home with a spotlessly clean, show-ready ride and not bring rain gear, I suggest you read about an ancient biker named Noah. You won't fare as well as he did.

Rain has been an issue for riders since the earliest days; it also plagued early automobile explorers since most early vehicles were open touring cars. There is nothing like getting soaked to the bone. Maybe add some mud for color, and then move through the air at high speeds. No matter if it is winter or summer, you will become chilled and uncomfortable.

So what does this have to do with food? Well, long before there were motor vehicles and roads, there was rain (read Noah again). Ancient man (could have been ancient women, it was a long time ago) invented soup. Soup is the surefire cure for those soaking wet, chilled to the bones times when you finally get smart enough to come in out of the rain. So when you break all the rules regarding rain prevention, just find a roadhouse and order some soup, or if you are still at home, cook some of these fine soups on a rainy day. You'll be glad you did.

Top of the Hill Grill, Vermont

632 Putney Road
Brattleboro, VT 05301
(802) 258-9178

Owner and chef Jon Julian says:

"This gumbo is obviously my adaptation of traditional recipes. My take on food in general and barbecue and gumbo in particular is that regional variations of the 'original' make them no less appealing or satisfying. A few years back, I went to Louisiana and spent six weeks in Cajun country hanging out in Cajun kitchens. Thanks goes to chef Pat Moulde of Lafayette, who told me I have to prepare food the way my customers want to eat it. As such, in my chicken and sausage gumbo, I have toned down the spice level and (I know this is blasphemous for some) left out the okra."

John uses filé powder to replace the thickening function that okra performs. Filé powder is made from ground sassafras leaves. Many large supermarkets carry it, especially in the South; you should also be able to order it from the many specialty food purveyors on the Internet.

Top of the Hill Grill Chicken and Sausage Gumbo

1 cup vegetable oil (I use a 75/25 canola/olive blend)
1 cup white flour
2 cups finely chopped onion
1 cup finely chopped celery
1 cup finely chopped green bell pepper
1 pound smoked sausage, coarsely chopped
½ pound andouille or tasso sausage, finely chopped
¼ teaspoon cayenne or chipotle pepper (optional)
3 small bay leaves
3 tablespoons Cajun spice (I use Tony Chachere's, or a no-salt or low-salt blend)
7 cups chicken broth, plus additional for adding during cooking
1 pound boneless chicken thighs, coarsely chopped
3 tablespoons finely chopped parsley
½ cup finely chopped green onion
1 teaspoon filé powder (optional)
8 cups cooked white rice

In a large Dutch oven, combine oil and flour. Stir constantly over medium heat for 10–15 minutes until the "roux," as it is called, is dark brown. Do *not* burn!

Add the onion, celery, and bell pepper to the pot and cook for 5 minutes, stirring often.

Add the sausages, cayenne or chipotle, bay leaves, 1 tablespoon of the Cajun spice, and the 7 cups broth. Stir well. Bring almost to a boil, then reduce heat and simmer uncovered for 20 minutes.

While the gumbo simmers, rub the chicken thighs with remaining 2 tablespoons Cajun spice to season them.

Add the chicken to the pot and simmer for 1 hour, adding more broth if necessary.

Skim fat if needed, and then stir in parsley, green onions, and filé powder.

Serve immediately over rice.

Makes 10 servings.

Jo Jo's Pizza & Soft Ice Cream, Ancram, New York

1015 Route 82
Ancram, NY 12502
(518) 851-6567

Here is another favorite choice of Susan Buck's when stopping at Jo Jo's Pizza & Soft Ice Cream. Susan related to me:

"For a couple of years, allergies forced me to forgo Stromboli. So, when those hundred miles contained excessive amounts of traffic, rain, or particularly bad drivers, Jo Jo's always offered comfort and nourishment like homemade minestrone, or a crisp salad with chicken. Even knowing that Harley Rendezvous is just another 75 miles ahead doesn't dissuade me from stopping for some refreshment.

"Riding motorcycles has been known to arouse the appetite. Within 20 miles of the Taconic Parkway and Route 82 are roads that spider west through the Adirondack Park and central New York State. This is some of the most beautiful riding in the country, and spring through fall, the farms, orchards, and mountain forests smell as good as they look. You're in deer country, as well as raccoon and skunk, so even if you think there's no one on the road, there might be. Enjoy the coffee, smile at the goats, and contemplate the next rolling hill."

I wish I had found Jo Jo's back in the day when I lived in the Big Apple, as I frequently rode in that area to get away from the city. It just goes to show that if you don't ask other riders were they find good grub and biker-friendly service, you will surely miss out on some good eats.

Mama's Minestrone

3 tablespoons extra virgin olive oil
3 cloves garlic, minced
1 large onion, peeled and coarsely chopped
4 stalks celery, coarsely chopped
5 carrots, peeled and coarsely chopped
5 potatoes, peeled and cut into 1-inch cubes
1 (4-ounce) can tomato paste
1 (16-ounce) can kidney beans, drained
1 (32-ounce) can vegetable broth
3 tablespoons chopped fresh basil
2 tablespoons dried oregano
1 tablespoon salt
2 cups cooked macaroni (optional; we use ziti that is cut in half)

Heat the olive oil in a large pot over medium heat. Add the garlic and onion and sauté for 5 to 10 minutes, or until tender. Do not brown, or the garlic becomes bitter.

Next, add the celery and carrots and continue sautéing for 5 minutes. Then mix in the potatoes, tomato paste, kidney beans, vegetable broth, and water. Stir well, bring to a boil, and reduce the heat to low. Mix in the basil, oregano, and salt and cook for 30 minutes, or until veggies are tender. If you like macaroni in your minestrone, add the cooked pasta about a minute before serving.

Makes 8 servings.

Doyle's Pub & Eatery, Richmond, Illinois

5604 Mill Street
Richmond, IL 60071
(815) 678-3623
www.doylespubrocks.com

You'll find Doyle's Pub & Eatery on U.S. Highway 12 in Richmond, Illinois, which is north of Chicago and almost at the state line with Wisconsin. Development of US 12 was begun in 1926, and the route runs east and west starting in Detroit, Michigan, and ending at Grey's Harbor in Washington State. This old blue line highway ran about 2,500 miles and has been bypassed by both Interstate 90 and 94, yet parts of the old road still pass through towns like Richmond with great biker-friendly eateries like Doyle's Pub.

If you visited Doyle's on any morning, you would likely find owner and chef Jeanne in the kitchen cooking up a storm, probably making one of her great soups. Jeanne says of making her Beef Barley soup:

"Start with a good beef stock; if you don't have beef stock on hand, then start with 2 gallons of water and 1 cup good beef base (I like LeGout) or prime rib bones or any beef bone from a butcher. This is a really nice, hearty soup that's a meal in itself. Did I tell you that my ninety-two-year-old dad grows all my spices, as well as my tomatoes, cukes, and green peppers in the summer? I freeze lots of his tomatoes and use them for sauces and soups throughout the winter!"

So when your travels take you north from Chicago, bypass the interstate crawl and spend some of the time you save at Doyle's Pub & Eatery.

Jeanne's Beef Barley Soup

½ gallon good beef stock
½ cup chopped onion
½ cup chopped celery
½ cup chopped carrots
2 cloves garlic, minced
1 bay leaf
1 tablespoon dried oregano
1 tablespoon dried basil
½ teaspoon black pepper
1 cup medium barley
½ cup diced tomatoes
1 cup good diced beef
   (I use prime rib or sirloin)
¼ cup good red wine
½ lemon

DOYLE'S PUB & EATERY

◼ Place the beef stock in a large pot over a high heat, and bring to a boil. Reduce the heat to medium and simmer for 30 minutes. Add the onion, celery, carrots, garlic, bay leaf, oregano, basil, black pepper, barley, tomatoes, and beef. Cook for at least 2 hours, stirring occasionally, until barley is cooked and tender.

◼ Add ¼ cup good red wine to soup (my rule of thumb is if you can't drink it, don't cook with it!). Squeeze the lemon juice into the soup and drop lemon half into the soup. Let soup set for half hour longer over a low heat. If too thick, add water.

◼ Serve with a nice glass of wine and garlic bread.

Makes about 1½ gallons.

Weisgerber's Cornerstone Pub & Restaurant, Baileys Harbor, Wisconsin

8123 State Highway 57
Baileys Harbor, WI 54202
(920) 839-9001
www.weisgerberscornerstonepub.com

I enjoyed a very nice meal here when I was last in Baileys Harbor. It was an in-season weekend evening, and the place was hopping. Despite the packed house, the wait was reasonable and well worth it. I had one of the homemade pizzas and some of the local Wisconsin favorite Leinenkugel beer. Next time I can get to Door County, I will be heading back for some more.

Sandy Weisgerber, owner and operator, tells me:

"Weisgerber's Cornerstone Pub has been in business for twenty-two years, family owned and operated by the Weisgerber family. Take a beautiful ride along the lakeshore on State Highway 57. It's located right across from the marina in Baileys Harbor. We have great fish plates and homemade pizzas. Stop in and try our 'Anniversary Burger' that is a big hit with the locals."

Seafood Chowder

4 (10¾ ounce) cans Campbell's clam chowder
2 cans milk (2% milk using the soup can as a measure)
½ cup chopped celery
½ cup diced onion
2 tablespoons parsley
1 teaspoon lemon pepper
1 teaspoon onion powder
1 teaspoon celery salt
½ cup salad shrimp
6 sticks imitation crab, cut into ½-inch pieces

In a large pot, combine the soup and milk and mix well. Add the celery, onion, parsley, lemon pepper, onion powder, celery salt, shrimp, and crab. Bring to a boil over medium heat. Reduce to low and allow to simmer for 5 to 10 minutes, stirring occasionally; be careful not to let it burn.

Makes 8–10 servings

- -

The Dillard House, Dillard, Georgia

1158 Franklin Street
Dillard, GA 30537
(706) 746-5348 or (800) 541-0671
www.dillardhouse.com

The Dillard House can be found in Dillard, Georgia, along part of the Old Dixie Highway. The modern road is part of the old numbered federal highway system, where U.S. Highways 23 and 441 run concurrently—these were parts of the eastern division of the Dixie Highway. US 441 runs from Lake City, Tennessee, to Miami, Florida, and US 23 runs from Mackinaw City to Jacksonville, Florida. Both roads pass through the Great Smoky Mountains area and near the southern end of the Blue Ridge Parkway in the western North Carolina/eastern Tennessee region. It's all great riding country, and you can easily get yourself over to the Dillard House for a taste of some traditional country food and hospitality. If you are in luck, they will be serving this tasty Cream of Broccoli Soup. Till then, while you are mapping out your route, make this dish at home. You'll become locally famous for it.

Dillard House Cream of Broccoli Soup

1 bunch fresh broccoli, finely diced
1 medium onion, finely diced
Salt and pepper to taste
3 tablespoons margarine
2 cups water
¼ cup cornstarch
1 quart heavy cream
1 tablespoon diced pimento

■ **In a medium-size saucepan, cook broccoli, onion, salt, and pepper with margarine and water until tender, about 10 to 15 minutes. Thicken with cornstarch dissolved in cold water. Add heavy cream and pimento. Bring back to a low boil, then serve.**

Makes 6 servings.

The Cottage Café, Cle Elum, Washington

911 East First Street
Cle Elum, WA 98922
(509) 674-2922

In March I performed my cooking shows at the 2008 Central Washington Home & Garden Show, which was held at the SunDome in Yakima, Washington. I left the work on this book to take an early-morning flight to Seattle, pick up a rental car, and drive east to the Yakima Valley. From my 4:00 a.m. North Carolina start to my arrival in Washington, all I had had to eat was coffee and the pitiful "breakfast" on the plane. What passes for airline food in first class these days is sad; just imagining what they served in coach that morning gives me the chills.

I made my way out of the morning rush hour traffic in Seattle and onto Interstate 90 East. By the time I had crossed over the Snoqualmie Pass in the mixed snow and rain, I was

starved. In short order I saw the sign for the Cottage Café in Cle Elum. The highway signage for Cle Elum promised easy off and on access to the interstate—just what the modern road user seeks, convenience. What I found was far better than the garish strips of service road America that are the destination of easy access. I found the small mountain town of Cle Elum, which was wearing the gray northwestern winter weather wrapped tight like Grandma's shawl. I also found the Cottage Café, with a very full parking lot on both sides and the front. There was a large area in back for eighteen-wheelers. I circled the building in the rain and got lucky with a spot just opening a short trot from the front door. Inside I found both shelter from the weather and the bustling warmth of patrons, cheery waitstaff, and the robust smell of coffee. I knew what I wanted: a real breakfast! I ordered pancakes and scrambled eggs. I almost ordered potatoes and a biscuit, too, and am glad I didn't. Why? Well, the pancakes alone would have been enough; I haven't seen such generously sized pancakes since I ordered them at a cafe on the Rembrandtplein in Amsterdam. The Dutch are known for their pancakes, which typically are served so large that they hang off the edges of the plate. The pancakes at the Cottage Café came close. I didn't measure, but they looked all of a foot in diameter, and they were delicious. They gave me the feeling of homey reassurance on a trip that had me almost 3,000 miles from home. A great breakfast served at 5,000 feet. But they serve more than breakfast and have been at it for a long time. While I thought I was taking a pause from the roadhouse cookbook, I had found a roadside gem. Here is their story in their own words–"Like Home for Hungry Travelers":

"The Cottage Café began in 1935, and there have been many changes over the years. In the '50s the grill was removed from behind the counter and an actual kitchen was installed. The '60s saw new restrooms, but you had to go outside to use them. The year 1980 brought a new owner and more seats to the north, and one of the best improvements yet—indoor restrooms.

"The Cottage sold again in 1986, and more changes . . . more seats, modern restrooms, in-house bakery, and the latest is the Fireside Cocktail Lounge.

"We cannot really own the Cottage Café; we are simply caretakers. Someday we will be gone, but the Cottage will remain—a haven for hungry travelers, families, and working people from all parts of the country."

Ben and Wanda Goldie, the present caretakers of the Cottage Café, had this to say about the Ham & Cheese Chowder: "We make our soups in 5-gallon steam kettles, but here is the recipe in a home kitchen size." Once you try this soup you will know why they make it in 5-gallon batches to conquer the cold Northwestern winters.

Ham & Cheese Chowder

4 tablespoons butter
1 cup chopped celery
1 cup chopped onion
2½ cups chopped ham
4 quarts diced potatoes

1 teaspoon chicken base
1⅛ cups dry nondairy creamer (4 ounces)
2 cups hot water
1¼ pounds American cheese
⅛ cup parsley

Melt the butter in a large soup pot over medium-high heat. Add the celery and sauté until tender, about 3 to 4 minutes. Add the onion, ham, potatoes, and enough water to cover and boil gently, stirring occasionally, until potatoes are done, about 30 minutes. Reduce heat to medium.

In a separate bowl, mix together the chicken base, creamer, and hot water, and then stir into the soup gently to avoid mashing the tender potatoes (you want chunks in the soup). Add the cheese a little at a time, stirring gently.

When all of the cheese is melted, the soup is done. Add the parsley, stir, and serve immediately.

Makes about a gallon of soup.

Nicky's Cruisin Diner, Bangor, Maine

957 Union Street
Bangor, ME 04401
(207) 942-3430
www.nickysdiner.com

Karen Day shared this diner's history with me:

"Nicky's Cruisin Diner started in the early 1970s as Nicky's Ice Cream Parlor. Owners Howie and Karen Day took over in November 1987. It was a few years later that they changed the name to Nicky's Cruisin Diner.

"The restaurant started with only five booths and eighteen stools out front. The inside wall used to be the location of another soda fountain, which remained until January 1994. That first renovation took out the counter and eighteen stools, and replaced them with the current small counter and booths. Three years later, in May 1997, the back dining room was completed, and thus began the collection of the many unique items on display now.

"Every Wednesday night from the end of May through the end of September, Nicky's is the place to be with Cruise Nite. Since 1992, people from all over this area bring their classic cars for good food, good company, and good music.

"The summer of 2005 brought a first for Nicky's Cruisin Diner. Along with the popular Cruise Nite for classic cars, Bike Nite began to accommodate those who drive on two wheels. This night is also a great time for good food, good company, good music, and bike games!

"Fall 2005 started with the popular loyalty program for all our loyal patrons, and winter 2006 marked the introduction of the well-received Seniority Program.

"Nicky's is always changing and evolving to become a place where anyone from any background can come for a great meal at reasonable prices with great company! Check us out at www.nickysdiner.com."

About this recipe, Karen said: "It is also great the next day after the flavors have really melded together! When I first started making the soup at home, I'd make it in the early afternoon to let it sit, then reheat it at dinner time. But if you need something really quick it is great for that, too; it can be done in less than one hour!"

Chicken Cajun Cheese Soup

2 tablespoons olive oil

2 chicken breasts, cut into bite-size pieces (about ½ pound)

1 medium onion, chopped fine

1 teaspoon minced garlic

½ teaspoon dried oregano

2 (16-ounce) cans or 1 (32-ounce) box of chicken or vegetable broth

1 (16-ounce) can diced tomatoes

1 to 2 teaspoons Cajun seasoning

2 yellow squash, sliced thin

2 medium zucchini, sliced thin

1 cup frozen corn

1½ cups Alfredo sauce

In a large (6- to 8-quart) pot, heat 1 tablespoon of the olive oil over medium heat, add the chicken, and sauté until no longer pink, about 15 to 20 minutes. Remove from the heat and transfer the chicken to a plate. Set aside.

In the same pot, add the remaining 1 tablespoon of olive oil and the onion and sauté until tender, about 5 minutes. You want the onion soft and opaque, not browned; it will finish cooking when the soup is simmering. Add the chicken, garlic, oregano, broth, tomatoes, Cajun seasoning, squash, zucchini, and corn. Bring to a gentle boil, then reduce heat to low and cook until the squash and zucchini are tender, about 15 to 20 minutes. Add the Alfredo sauce and finish heating for about 5 minutes.

Makes approximately 6 servings.

Amish Acres, Nappanee, Indiana

1600 West Market Street
Nappanee, IN 46550
(574) 773-4188 or (800) 800-4942
www.amishacres.com

Janis Logsdon, Marketing and Group Sales Director for Amish Acres, was kind enough to share three recipes that speak to the spirit of the experience and fine meal you will have if you

Amish Acres Famous Bean Soup AMISH ACRES

visit Amish Acres in Nappanee, Indiana. Here is what she shared: "The following recipe has been published in our own *Amish Acres Recipes Cookbook* (Nappanee, Indiana, 2001). Also following is a portion from the introduction in that cookbook:

"Amish Acres in Nappanee, Indiana, is the only Old Order Amish farmstead in America listed on the National Register of Historic Places. For over three of its thirteen decades the farm has been in a state of preservation for the purpose of interpreting Amish culture to an unfamiliar world. Among the traditions of these people who adhere to the patterns of life from seventeenth-century European peasant culture are the food habits of a time and place whose influence on American cuisine has been pervasive to the point of going unnoticed.

"Amish Acres has served an iron kettle of piping hot bean soup as its first course for the award-winning Threshers Dinner for over thirty years. Much success with your own bean soup, and please come visit Amish Acres and indulge in the Thresher's Dinner—from your first spoonful of bean soup to the last bite of crumb topping on our homemade shoofly pie."

- -

Amish Acres Famous Bean Soup

1 pound soup beans
1 ham bone
½ cup chopped onion
½ teaspoon celery salt

½ teaspoon seasoning salt
Dash garlic salt
Salt and pepper to taste

Soak beans in water overnight. (When using dried beans you must sort and rinse them first. As a product that is often packaged by machine, small pebbles or dirt clumps will often be included. While their presence is normal, you don't want to cook with pebbles and dirt.)

Drain, add fresh water, and cook slowly with the ham bone for 2 hours. Add onion, celery salt, seasoning salt, garlic salt, and salt and pepper.

Remove ham bone, trim off any meat, and return to pot. Add ham bits to pot and simmer for 1 hour.

Makes 15–16 servings.

- -

The Time Warp Tea Room, Knoxville, Tennessee

1209 North Central Street
Knoxville, TN 37917
(865) 524-1155
www.timewarpvmc.org

This taco soup recipe is a Time Warp Bike Night special. From their Web site, here is the history of the Time Warp Tea Room and the rider's club that gathers there:

"There had always been a group of vintage-motorcycle folks in Knoxville, and some gathered on the old Thursday bike nights in the Old City when Biker Rags still had a location on Central. Over beers and wings at the now-defunct Spicy's, we talked about forming a vintage-motorcycle club to give all the talented and interesting moto-characters in Knoxville a reason to gather.

"Nothing organized really came of it, but the idea never really went away, and we'd discuss it at events like the swap meets at the (also defunct) Farmers Market. Then one fall day in 2002 Dan Moriarty opened the Time Warp Tea Room and encouraged us to park our old bikes on the sidewalk. Via (also defunct) Speedvision's Two-Wheeled-Tuesday, Tuesday evenings became the atypical motorcyclist's hangout, and the club was born at the big round table soon after.

"There were but a handful of members at first, but with the emphasis on a maximum of fun and a minimum of administrative burden, the TWVMC grew quickly, despite minor skirmishes over checking accounts, smoking at meetings, and skulls on T-shirts. Some amazingly talented people call themselves Time Warpers, help each other out with our old heaps, and have a great time along the way. Happy Holler is home base, and we have chapters in Columbia, Tennessee, upstate New York, and Boise, Idaho."

It just goes to prove that riders are a fun-loving group who just want to get together and socialize over good food and around their favorite rides.

Riders enjoying Route 14A, a South Dakota National Forest Service Scenic By-way near Cheyenne Crossing, South Dakota, during the 2006 Sturgis Rally and Races BILL HUFNAGLE

Taco Soup

3 pounds lean ground beef
1 large onion, minced
3 packages taco seasoning (1.25-ounce McCormick brand)
1 package ranch dressing mix (1-ounce Hidden Valley brand mix)
3 (10-ounce) cans Rotel tomatoes
1 (28-ounce) large can diced tomatoes
3 (16-ounce) cans pinto beans, drained
3 (11-ounce) cans niblet corn, drained
1½ cups water
Fritos brand corn chips
Shredded lettuce
Diced tomatoes
Shredded cheddar cheese
Sour cream

In a large pot, combine the beef and onion and cook over medium-high heat for 10 to 15 minutes or until the beef is browned. Add the taco seasoning, ranch dressing mix, tomatoes, beans, corn, and water, and bring to a boil. Reduce the heat to low and simmer 30 minutes.

Serve over corn chips or crushed taco shells and top with shredded lettuce, diced tomatoes, shredded cheddar, and sour cream.

Makes about 20 servings.

6

Salads

For me, any meal other than breakfast should have a salad of some type served with it. Fresh greens and garden vegetables are both tasty and very good for your health. Often when I have a choice of a good salad bar, that is what I will choose for lunch and/or dinner. Of course, I do like to inspect it first for freshness and to ensure there is enough variety. Even when my main course is salad, I like to enjoy a little of the traditional side salads, especially coleslaw and potato salad. Would you like salad with your salad, sir? Yes, of course!

Some lunch dishes, like sandwiches, are often served with a choice of slaw or fries, or maybe both, if you are lucky. Then there is barbecue. Think of the classic pulled pork barbecue sandwich served on a roll with the slaw right on top of the pork and sauce. It wouldn't be the same without it. In this chapter you will find coleslaws, potato salad, an entree-caliber chicken salad, and more. So load up on these salads—good taste and good health in the same dish. You just can't beat that recipe any meal of the day.

The Red Planet Diner, Sedona, Arizona

1655 W Highway 89A
Sedona, AZ 86336
(928) 282-6070

My buddy Josh Placa recommended the Red Planet Diner in his hometown of Sedona, Arizona:

"Exploring the eerie desert frontier of the Southwest by motorcycle can build up a mighty hunger. After a long, hard day down the dusty trail, a good place to rest and refuel is the unearthly Red Planet Diner. Spaceships and various aliens hang from the walls and ceilings of this Sedona, Arizona eatery."

This light salad can either be a side salad or turned into a main course by topping it with one of the optional protein sources listed (adjust the ingredient amounts to suit your dining mission). Try replicating it at home in your food preparation module—that is spaceman talk for *whip it up in your kitchen.* Then next time you are in Sedona you can try the original while cooling your thrusters at the Red Planet Diner.

Solar Salad

Romaine lettuce or Spring Mix	*Options:*
walnut quarters	steak strips (diner favorite)
crumbled Gorgonzola cheese	chicken strips
Solar Dressing (recipe is in the Travel Trailer chapter)	salmon

▨ **Place the Romaine or Spring Mix in a salad bowl. Sprinkle with the walnuts and Gorgonzola cheese. If desired top off the salad with your choice of optional proteins. Serve with Solar Dressing.**

Makes 1 serving.

Weisgerber's Cornerstone Pub & Restaurant, Baileys Harbor, Wisconsin

8123 State Highway 57
Baileys Harbor, WI
(920) 839-9001

I first ventured into Door County for the opening of a new bookstore called Novel Idea's, where I performed some of my cooking shows. Pat Palmer and his daughter Michelle, who own and operate the store, recommended Weisgerber's Cornerstone Pub. The pub is located just up the road (Wisconsin Highway 57) in the same town, Baileys Harbor, Wisconsin. This is a fun place that was very friendly, and the food was great. Here is the recipe for their Tri-Color Cold Pasta Salad. Try it at home, and it would make a great pack-along salad for a picnic lunch.

Tri-Color Cold Pasta Salad

2 (1-pound) boxes tri-color noodles
3 cups vinegar
3 cups sugar
1½ cups vegetable oil
1 tablespoon celery seed
½ cup diced green peppers

½ cup diced onions
½ cup diced tomatoes
½ cup diced cucumbers
¼ cup sliced black olives

   Fill a large pot with water, place over high heat, and bring to a boil. Add the noodles and cook to al dente according to package directions. Drain and place in cold water.

   While the noodles are cooling, combine in a blender the vinegar, sugar, oil, and celery seed and mix well. Drain the noodles and transfer to a large mixing bowl. Add the green peppers, onions, tomatoes, cucumbers, and olives. Pour the vinegar mixture over all the ingredients and toss well to coat. Cover and refrigerate for 5 hours before serving. Serve chilled. It is even more excellent the second day.

Makes about 20 servings.

Pig 'N Steak, Madison, Virginia

313 Washington Street
Madison, VA 22727
(540) 948-3130
www.pigandsteak.com

Slaw is one of my favorite side salads; especially in the hot summer months, and during the winter it can turn a simple sandwich into an indoor picnic. It is a good source of fiber, delightfully crunchy, yet creamy and sweet with just a light tang—a darn near perfect combination. Little wonder it is a Southern favorite and a staple with barbecue. Many barbecue places guard their slaw recipe as much as their sauces and "Q" secrets. So consider yourself honored that this recipe has been shared with you. And say a word of thanks to both the man who recommended Pig 'N Steak and the folks there who shared their recipe.

"My name is Dick Marshall. We met just before one of your presentations at Waugh Enterprise HD in Orange, Virginia, several years ago. I am the fellow who bought over $200 worth of books that you autographed for me, and you kindly gave me an apron. As many people as you meet, you probably don't remember, and no one could blame you!

     "Anyway, I wanted to suggest a 'roadhouse' for your consideration in the upcoming book. The place is the Pig 'N Steak in Madison, Virginia, just off Route 29 between Charlottesville and Culpeper. The quality of the food there is outstanding, and prices are reasonable. They

Exterior of Pig 'N Steak, Madison, Virginia PIG 'N STEAK

have a custom pit smoker out back that is large enough to hold a small club meeting inside! The 'small' order of fries is huge and only $1.85. It is all my wife and I can eat to share one. I have never seen the large order. The barbecue is outstanding, as are the steaks. How many 'roadhouses' do you see that have Bass Ale on draft?"

Dick, thank you for both the recommendation and making my last book a big part of your Christmas gifting! From my talks with John and his team at Pig 'N Steak, I can tell they not only serve good food, they do it with true Southern hospitality, which is one of the true secrets of presenting a memorable meal. Here are a few words from their Web site:

"Our customers enjoy homemade coleslaw, potato salad, and baked beans. We cook everything homemade. Our salad dressings are made fresh, and you can taste the freshness every time."

Creamy Vinegar Slaw

2½ cups sugar
4 cups mayonnaise
Scant teaspoon Nature's Seasoning
1 teaspoon celery salt
1 cup cider vinegar
6 pounds cabbage, coarsely grated

In a medium mixing bowl (use a bowl made of a nonreactive material like glass, non-staining plastic, or stainless steel), combine the sugar, mayonnaise, Nature's Seasoning, celery salt, and vinegar, and blend together well. Place the cabbage in a large bowl, cover with the dressing, and toss together well. Cover and refrigerate for at least 1 hour before serving. Serve chilled.

Makes about 1 gallon.

Here is an except from the official Pig 'N Steak Web site: "Those who know the owner, John E. Lohr, personally can understand why he has the recipe and technique for barbecue down to a science. He started out cooking hogs and pigs on a grill for private parties over thirty-five years ago. He built up quite a reputation many years before he ventured inside and opened the Pig 'N Steak." When I asked John about this, he told me: "We celebrated our twentieth anniversary on April 1, 2007. I began cooking hogs for friends about thirty-five years ago and love to cook. I worked for years at my parents' grocery store, and I was familiar with working with the public and food vendors, so it was a natural move into the restaurant business. I still love the business, and I still love to cook and entertain."

That is what you really want to find when you get hungry while out on the old roads exploring America: a good place to eat where folks love what they do and want to share their culinary expertise with you. Good food and down-home hospitality are waiting for you at places like Pig 'N Steak; all you need to do is ride on over, and John and his crew will do you right. Until then, try the following chicken salad recipe at home while you map out your trip.

Chicken Salad

5 pounds cooked boneless chicken, cooled and coarsely chopped
2½ cups medium-chopped celery
4 cups mayonnaise
1½ cups sweet pickle relish
1 tablespoon Nature's Seasoning
½ tablespoon celery salt
1 tablespoon Old Bay Seasoning

In a large mixing bowl, combine chicken and celery; toss together well. Add the mayonnaise, pickle relish, Nature's Seasoning, celery salt, and Old Bay Seasoning and mix thoroughly. Cover and refrigerate for at least 1 hour before serving. Serve chilled.

Makes about ¾ gallon.

The Farmer's Daughter, Chuckey, Tennessee

7700 Erwin Highway
Chuckey, TN 37641
(423) 257-4650
www.thefarmersdaughterrestaurant.com

Tammy Blankenship, from my local ABATE/CBA chapter, recommended the Farmer's Daughter to me at a meeting. As other folks in the chapter became aware and spoke to me about this book, several also made the same recommendation. Talk about word-of-mouth advertising—I must have gotten close to a dozen referrals to include this country-style restaurant. Here is a bit from their Web site:

"For more than three years, the Farmer's Daughter Restaurant has specialized in bringing the wholesomeness of a homemade meal to the table of thousands of hungry customers. Located

in Chuckey, Tennessee, the Farmer's Daughter strives to provide excellent cuisine and service. A variety of meats and vegetables are served, choices changing with each week. The whole family is sure to enjoy a visit to the Farmer's Daughter."

Dan and Rachel Tyson open the Farmer's Daughter only on Friday, Saturday, and Sunday. They serve family-style, and it is all you can eat (excluding dessert). They offer a true down-home country-style dining experience just like in the halcyon days of a bygone era.

When I approached Dan about sharing some recipes for the book, he was more than gracious and gave me three. He then went on to provide me with many recommendations to other fine old-timey places that serve food the way he and Rachel like it—just like they serve it. Thank you, Dan and Rachel!

I am sure you will enjoy this simple yet tasty Cucumbers and Onions recipe.

Cucumbers and Onions

4 large cucumbers, peeled and sliced
¼ cup salt
Ice water
2 medium onions, sliced

1 quart vinegar
1¼ cups sugar
1 cup water

Place cucumbers in a large bowl, sprinkle salt over them, and add ice water to cover. Let stand one hour. Drain and add onions. In a large saucepan, combine remaining ingredients and bring to a boil. Boil 5 minutes. Pour hot mixture over vegetables. Refrigerate and use within 24 hours.

Makes 10–12 servings.

When you serve this delicious potato salad you may chill it first. Or the old-timey way of doing it is to serve it immediately so it is still just a little warm, which is it how Dan said his mom served it.

Finally, for the Farmer's Daughter Chess Pie recipe, go to the Desserts chapter.

Mom's Potato Salad

6 medium potatoes
1 large dill pickle, finely chopped
2 eggs, hard-cooked and chopped
1 onion, chopped
½ cup vinegar
½ teaspoon celery seed
1 teaspoon mustard
1 teaspoon salt
½ cup sugar

▪ Cook potatoes until tender in boiling salted water; drain and let cool enough to handle. Peel and cube potatoes. In a large bowl, combine the potatoes with the remaining ingredients, mixing gently.

Makes 6–8 servings.

Peaks of Otter Lodge, Bedford, Virginia

Mile marker 86 of the Blue Ridge Parkway
P.O. Box 489
Bedford, VA 24523
(540) 586-1081 (or 800-542-5927)
Fax (540) 586-4420
www.peaksofotter.com

The Peak of Otter, located at mile marker 86 of the Blue Ridge Parkway (BRP) in Virginia. is one of my favorite stopping points along the northern section of the BRP and a place I often recommend to friends who are motoring to visit me from the Northeast. While most of the lodging and eateries along the BRP are only open from spring to fall, the Peaks of Otter Lodge and Restaurant are open all year long.

Ron Stull was kind enough to share this long-time favorite recipe from their restaurant. It makes either a great start to a home-style country meal or a light dessert. You will enjoy it all year long at home or better yet at the very special mountain setting that is the Peaks of Otter Lodge.

Peaks of Otter Fruit Salad

20 ounces whipping cream
6 tablespoons powdered sugar
8 ounces cream cheese
1 (36-ounce) can crushed pineapple, drained, reserve juice
1 (36-ounce) can peaches, cut into ½-inch pieces and well drained (at least 1 hour)
1 (36-ounce) can pears cut into ½-inch pieces and well drained (at least 1 hour)
6 ounces miniature marshmallows
16 ounces maraschino cherries, well drained and cut in half
5 ounces mayonnaise

▨ Whip the whipping cream until it's rather stiff, and add powdered sugar. Set aside in the refrigerator.

▨ Place the cream cheese in mixing bowl and commence beating. Add the drained pineapple juice. Scrape the sides of the bowl and check cream cheese mixture that there are no lumps.

▨ Add all pineapple, peaches, pears, marshmallows, cherry halves, cream cheese mixture, whipped cream, and mayonnaise, and fold all together thoroughly.

▨ If you like coconut, add 1 cup sweetened shredded coconut. Feel free to play or experiment with this recipe to better fit your taste.

Makes 20 Servings.

7

Main Dishes

At the end of a long day on the road, your lungs filled to capacity for hours upon hours with clean fresh air, and what do you think you develop? An appetite as big as a freeway, that's what. That fresh air is the main culprit. It probably doesn't help that as the day rolls on toward dinnertime your body just naturally wants to be nourished. You are a creature of habit, aren't you? Then there are the aromas of food cooking that are wafting through the air. It is hard to ride anywhere that is inhabited near dinnertime and not encounter the scents of cooking.

You find your lodgings for the night, park and unpack your trusty motorcycle (sports car if you must), doff your leathers and boots, and change into something more comfortable, for walking or dining. Something preferably with an adjustable waist, or just loose enough to accommodate a nice meal. You have earned it. A day of piloting a motorcycle in traffic can be both exciting and sometimes hard, dangerous work, mostly because some folks just don't respect a motorcycle rider's equal rights on the road. Or maybe you were lucky and traveled almost deserted roads, back roads, or stretches of the lost blue line highways. Places bypassed by the interstate, where the only traffic is laid-back local folks who are not caught up by the hurry-up mania of the fast-lane life.

Whatever the day's adventures were, it is time for dinner, and the focus of dinner is the entree or main dish. Yes, something hearty and satisfying, rich in protein and full of robust flavors, or maybe you want your protein on the lighter side, with delicate flavors. It is in here, from pot roast or meat loaf to chicken fried steak or fried catfish, and more; the choices are yours, so wander into the kitchen and choose. To have this amount of choices from this many great roadhouses would require a food court that was nationwide!

Amish Acres' nationally famous Thresher's Dinner, a family-style feast of Amish country favorites AMISH ACRES

Lancaster's Fine Dining, Bloomington, Illinois

513 North Main Street
Bloomington, IL 61701
(309) 827-3333

Back in the glory days of Route 66, it passed through Bloomington, Illinois, where it intersected with U.S. Highway 51. In that day, that made Bloomington a big crossroads town and a great place to stop for a meal and gas or overnight stay. Nowadays Route 66 has been replaced with Interstate 55, and US 51 replaced by Interstate 35 north of town; those two interstates, along with Interstate 74, bypass around town. Still, Bloomington is a great place to stop and slow down. In the middle of town you will find a truly fine dining experience at Lancaster's. They serve excellent gourmet food—Emily Post would have loved this place during her cross-country adventure. Stop in and give them a try, and tell them Biker Billy said Alright!

This recipe they shared is a personal favorite of mine. When I visit my friends at Chuck's Harley-Davidson in Bloomington, Winnie Feken (president and founder) and I always try to share a meal at Lancaster's.

Lancaster's Butternut Squash Alfredo

The Squash
1 butternut squash, halved lengthwise and seeded
2 tablespoons melted butter
1 teaspoon ground nutmeg
1 teaspoon ground cinnamon

The Alfredo Sauce
1 cup heavy cream
½ teaspoon ground nutmeg
½ teaspoon ground cinnamon
¼ teaspoon ground cayenne pepper
1 teaspoon salt
½ teaspoon ground white pepper
½ cup crumbled Gorgonzola cheese, plus extra for garnish
½ cup grated Parmesan cheese, plus extra for garnish
½ cup finely shredded mozzarella cheese, plus extra for garnish
1 pound fettuccine, cooked al dente according to package directions

▧ **Preheat the oven to 400°F.**

▧ **Place the squash halves cut side up in a large baking pan. Brush with the butter and sprinkle the tops with the nutmeg and cinnamon. Bake for 45 to 60 minutes or until the squash is tender. Remove from oven and allow to cool to room temperature. Scoop out the centers, taking care to leave the shells intact for later use. Place the squash in a blender and puree.**

In a large saucepan over medium heat, combine the squash, heavy cream, nutmeg, cinnamon, cayenne, salt, and pepper. Stir well and simmer for 5 minutes, stirring often. Reduce the heat to low and add the Gorgonzola, Parmesan, and mozzarella. Stir well. Simmer gently, stirring often, until the Alfredo sauce thickens.

Ladle the sauce over the hot pasta and toss together. Divide the pasta between the two squash shells and sprinkle with the extra cheeses. Bake at 400°F until the cheese melts and is slightly browned. Serve immediately.

Makes 2 servings.

Chuck's Harley-Davidson, Bloomington, Illinois

2027 Ireland Grove Road
Bloomington, IL 61704
(309) 662-1648
www.chucksharley-dav.com

Chuck's Harley-Davidson, Inc. is located on Ireland Grove Road in Bloomington, Illinois, not far from the original Route 66; you will see their tall sign from Business Route 55. Chuck and Winnie founded the dealership in December 1971. Chuck has sadly been gone since 1980, which made Winnie one of very few woman to solely own and operate a Harley-Davidson dealership in those days. It is wonderful to see how they do so many things at the dealership to honor Chuck's memory; both he and Winnie always were and still are dedicated to their customers.

I have known Winnie since we met down under during the Harley-Davidson Open Road Tour in Sydney, Australia. Winnie and the whole family at Chuck's are lovers of good food and know the meaning of hospitality. Their open houses are famous for the great home-cooked foods and other delicious goodies they serve. Stop by and visit them when you are in the area. Make sure to ask them where the good places to eat are; they know the area and great food real well!

- -

Chuck's Harley-Davidson "Shop" Pot Roast

6 pounds lean beef rump roast, cut into 3-inch cubes
6 cloves garlic, sliced
1 tablespoon dried parsley leaves
1 tablespoon dried celery flakes
½ teaspoon ground black pepper
¼ teaspoon dried thyme leaves
1 bunch celery, cut into 1-inch pieces
1 pound carrots, peeled and cut into 1-inch pieces
8 potatoes, cut in half with skins left on
1 large cabbage, cut into eighths

▨ **Preheat oven to 450°F.**

▨ **Line a large roaster pan with extra-heavy-duty foil. Place the beef in the roaster. Sprinkle with the garlic, parsley, celery flakes, black pepper, and thyme. Add the celery, carrots, potatoes, and cabbage. Wrap tightly with foil and cover with the roaster lid. Bake for 1 hour. Reduce heat to 325 and bake for 2 hours. Let rest for 20 minutes and serve.**

Makes 10–12 servings.

- -

Home Folk's Diner, Asheville, North Carolina

**1459 Merrimon Avenue
Asheville, NC 28804
(828) 281-3613**

The Home Folk's Diner in Asheville, North Carolina is where my local ABATE/CBA (American Bikers Aimed Toward Education/Concerned Bikers Association) chapter has its monthly meeting. They close the restaurant early on the second Tuesday of every month for the meeting. That is what you call biker friendly! Wayne and Jessica Glass are the third owners of the restaurant, which first opened its doors in 1998. Having his own restaurant was a lifelong dream of Wayne's. He had worked in restaurant management for ten years prior to buying the Home Folk's Diner. Together Wayne and Jessica serve up some great down-home southern cooking—just like momma made.

You'll find the Home Folk's Diner along U.S. Business Route 23 in Asheville, North Carolina. Stop in and enjoy some good cooking and pick up a copy of the ABATE/CBA newsletter while you're there.

Home Folk's Diner Meatloaf

6 large eggs
1 tablespoon salt
1 tablespoon pepper
1 tablespoon garlic powder
¼ cup Worcestershire sauce
5 pounds hamburger meat
½ loaf of bread, crumbled
1 cup diced onions
1 cup diced green peppers
Ketchup

Preheat oven to 350°F.

In a medium mixing bowl, combine the eggs, salt, pepper, garlic powder, and Worcestershire sauce. Whisk together well.

In a large mixing bowl, combine the hamburger, bread crumbs, onions, and green peppers; mix together. Add the egg mixture and mix until completely combined.

Transfer to a 13x9x2-inch loaf pan; cover the top with a layer of ketchup. Cover with foil. Bake for 1½ hours, remove from oven, and drain juices.

Return to oven and bake uncovered for 20 more minutes.

Makes 10–15 servings.

Cheyenne Crossing Store and Café, Lead, South Dakota

Junctions of Highways 14A and S85
21415 U.S. Highway 14A
Spearfish Canyon
Lead, SD 57754
(605) 584-3510
www.cheyennecrossing.org

In 2006 Harley-Davidson hired me to go to the Sturgis Rally in South Dakota and write a daily blog of my adventures there with a food-related theme for their Web coverage of the rally. With thanks to Harley-Davidson, what follows is an excerpt from that blog:

"After spending the early half of my day doing the rally shuffle all over downtown Sturgis I was growing weary of the crowds and walking. Besides I had bought a few goodies and my saddlebags were getting kinda full so it was time to ride. Funny how for some folks the appeal of major rallies like Sturgis is hanging around town all day and night. I have friends who get there early to find a good parking spot and then just hang out and watch the people. Now that may be fun and they do have some interesting photos to show for their time, but I can only take so much of standing and watching. This is a motorcycle rally, and that means riding, especially since the true draw of this place, for like-minded folks and me, is the great roads and scenery. So it was on the bike and off for one of my favorite Sturgis rides. Heading out of town going west on Lazelle Street aka Route 34, I picked up I-90 west and headed for Spearfish Canyon, exit 14, turned left at the top of the ramp, then across the bridge and right at the T-intersection onto Route 14A, which is a South Dakota (National Forest Service) Scenic Byway. This is a beautiful twisty canyon road, with gray, pink, and brown-colored vertical rock formations rising up from the canyon bottom amidst the ever-present ponderosa pines whose dark green is so deep it sometimes makes the hills appear black, giving the region its name. Along with the delightful curves of good asphalt you will find a lot of scenic places to stop, among them Bridal Veil Falls and Roughlock Falls—the latter has a nice trail to hike along Little Spearfish Creek. Of course there are plenty of unnamed places to pull over and admire the creek, the hills, and the many other bikes sharing this ride.

"Approaching the juncture of routes 14A and 85 I spied a café and general store, which

Cheyenne Crossing Store and Café, Lead, South Dakota during the 2006 Sturgis Rally and Races BILL HUFNAGLE

looked like a good place to stop and explore. I parked the bike in the hard-packed earth and stone lot and dismounted, going in search of something cold to drink. The Cheyenne Crossing Store and Café, Junctions of Highways 14A and S85, Spearfish Canyon, and (605) 584-3510, offers both indoor and outdoor seating at which to enjoy your beverages and vittles. After acquiring an appropriate beverage I found a shaded perch to watch the bikes slow for the stop sign on 14A coming out of Spearfish Canyon. It made a good place to rest and enjoy the rolling bike show. After a while when my thirst was quenched I realized that I was a touch hungry and decided to go into the store to buy a snack. While perusing the items in the store I saw the waitress bring a couple of colorful plates of food to a table in the attached dining room. My hunger shifted gears and I decided I needed to have a seat and investigate the menu. After a longish wait at the sign that said PLEASE WAIT TO BE SEATED, I asked the nice lady at the store's register if she could seat me. Seeing that I was solo she told me to sit anywhere I pleased.

Shortly, Dave, who I later discovered was one of the cooks, brought me a menu. I immediately saw what I wanted, a veggie Indian taco, which is a piece of Indian fry bread, smothered in a tasty bean sauce with a thick Pico de Giao sauce, lettuce, black olives, shredded cheddar cheese, and a healthy dollop of cream cheese. They come in two sizes, small for $6.99 and large for $9.99. Having overheard the folks talking at the table whose orders I had seen delivered, I ordered the small. The large plates two of those guys were working on seemed like more than I could eat. When the waitress Julie brought my small Indian Taco, I was glad I ordered that size; it was plenty. And it was plenty good too, the fry bread being rich and light, a nice combo, and the taco ingredients were yummy too. Fry bread is a Native American food developed in the 1800s when the Indian Nations were forced onto reservations; deprived of their natural food sources and supplied by the government with wheat flour and lard. In 2005 it was named the official state bread of South Dakota, the same year it was also implicated as a possible cause of obesity and diabetes in Native Americans. Enjoying it a few times while on vacation won't do you any harm, and it is interesting to sample something close to local cuisine. The store there also had packages of Indian Fry Bread Mix that you could take home as a souvenir. This was a very pleasant stop along my ride, low key and relaxing, making for a nice pause from the rally crowds. While I had to wait for a table, it was not as long as some places will be during this busy week, and from what I could tell the small staff was handling the volume very well. If you ride Spearfish Canyon, and you should, consider a stop at the Cheyenne Crossing Store and Café."

I enjoyed that Indian Taco so much I had to get the recipe for you. So I called and asked David Brueckner, who owns and operates The Cheyenne Crossing Store and Café, and he was kind enough to share the recipe. The Cheyenne Crossing was established in 1878 as a stagecoach stop, making it a truly old-time roadhouse. They sell the Woodenknife Brand of Indian Fry Bread Mix, which is used in this recipe; you could serve this on tortillas or in taco shells, but you would be missing the true experience. Another hint from David: "We use dried black beans from Ortega."

World-Famous Indian Taco—Vegetarian Style

1 (12 to 16) ounce package dried
   black beans
1 tablespoon canola oil
¼ cup diced onions
⅓ cup diced green chilies
¼ cup chopped finely celery
½ cup diced tomatoes, fresh or canned
¼ cup diced green peppers
½ teaspoon cumin (more if you like)
2 tablespoons Ortega taco seasoning
2 tablespoons light chili powder
2 tablespoons salsa or picante sauce
1 tablespoons fresh parsley, finely chopped

1 tablespoons garlic powder or fresh
   crushed garlic
Salt and pepper to taste
Dash of cayenne pepper, or to your taste
   (we like a little zing)
Tomato juice
Indian Fry Bread Mix
Lettuce (we use red leaf)
Minced red onions
Black olives
Shredded cheddar cheese
Sour cream
Sliced jalapenos

■ Soak the black beans as recommended on the package. Drain and reserve half the soaking water; measure the reserved water, as you will need an equal measure of tomato juice.

■ Heat the canola oil in a large sauté pan over medium heat. Add the onions, green chilies, celery, tomatoes (save some to top taco), and green peppers, and sauté until tender about 5 to 7 minutes. Then add the cumin, taco seasoning, light chili powder, salsa, garlic, parsley, salt, pepper, and cayenne pepper, and stir well.

■ Add the beans and reserved liquid and tomato juice. Simmer the beans over low heat until they thicken nicely; adjust your spices as needed to taste.

■ Once the beans have thickened, prepare the Indian Fry Bread Mix according to package directions.

■ Place a piece of fry bread on a plate, cover with some bean mixture; add the lettuce, tomatoes, onions, black olives, shredded cheddar, and a dollop of sour cream—jalapeños if you like. Enjoy!

Makes 4 servings.

Ron Jillian's, Hampton, New Hampshire

822 Lafayette Road
Hampton, NH 03842
(603) 929-9966

Ron Jillian's is located on U.S. Route 1 in the historic seacoast town of Hampton, New Hampshire. US 1 in Hampton is paralleled on the west by Interstate 95 and along the coast by New Hampshire Highway 1A. If you are making the annual pilgrimage to Laconia Bike Week in June, it is a nice detour (and a short one for many) to visit the New Hampshire coast. The nice folks at Seacoast Harley-Davidson, who highly recommended Ron Jillian's, usually have some fun stuff going on that week. A nice combination: seashore and mountains in one rally week.

- -

Mussels Bianco over Linguine

2 ounces Pomace oil (you may substitute extra virgin olive oil)
2 tablespoons chopped fresh garlic
1 pound fresh Prince Edward Island mussels
2 teaspoons oregano
2 ounces whole unsalted butter
1 cup dry white wine
¼ pound linguine, cooked according to package directions

In a large sauté pan, heat the oil over low heat, add the garlic, and sauté until soft, about 2 to 3 minutes. Add the mussels and oregano and toss, coating all mussels. Add the butter and wine, turn heat to high, and cover. Steam mussels until open, about 2 to 3 minutes. Serve over linguine.

Makes 1 serving.

- -

Biker Billy SARAH K. NIX

Blue Willow Inn, Social Circle, Georgia

294 North Cherokee Road (GA 11)
P.O. Box 465
Social Circle, GA 30025
(770) 464-2131 or (800) 552-8813
www.bluewillowinn.com

You'll find the Blue Willow Inn about 50 miles east of Atlanta in the small town of Social Circle, Georgia. It is located on Georgia Highway 11. Take exit 98 on Interstate 20, and when you make your way to the Blue Willow Inn you can slip back in time and enjoy the down-home cooking and hospitality that the South is famous for. Louis and Billie Van Dyke shared a few recipes from their delightful cookbook *The Blue Willow Inn Bible of Southern Cooking* (Rutledge Hill Press, 2005).

Here is what they say about this classic Southern dish. "A true favorite of our guests, Chicken and Dumplings is served at almost every meal at the Blue Willow Inn Restaurant. Although it may take a while to prepare, the final product is worth the effort. It is great on a cold winter night. Add a salad and some crackers or toast for a complete meal."

Blue Willow Chicken and Dumplings

1 (3- to 4-pound) broiler-fryer chicken
2 cups self-rising flour
1 teaspoon salt
¼ cup shortening
½ cup (1 stick) melted butter
2 teaspoons black pepper

In a stockpot on medium-high heat, place the chicken in 2 quarts water. Cook until done, about 1 hour. Remove the chicken from the pot, reserving the chicken broth. Cool the chicken. After the chicken has cooled, remove the bones, skin, and fat. Cut the chicken into bite-size pieces and set aside.

In a medium-size mixing bowl, combine the flour and salt. Cut the shortening into the flour mixture until the mixture forms coarse crumbs. Add ¼ cup cold water and mix well with your hands to form a dough.

Over medium-high heat, bring the chicken broth back to a slow boil. Do not boil rapidly. With floured hands, pinch off pieces of the dough about the size of a quarter and drop them into the slowly boiling chicken broth. Gently stir the broth after adding several pieces of dough. Repeat until all the dumpling mix has been used and stir gently. Add the butter and black pepper. Stir gently.

Add the chicken pieces, turn the heat to low, and allow the mixture to simmer for 8 to 10 minutes. Serve in soup bowls.

Makes about 10 servings.

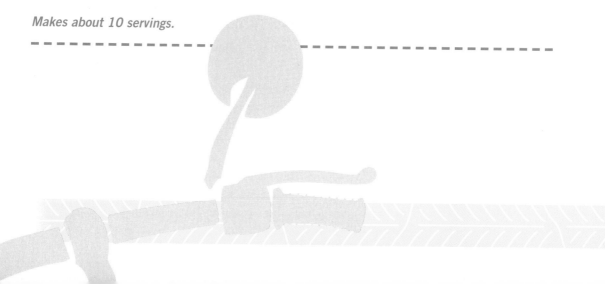

Storm's Drive-In, Burnet, Texas

Storm's Restaurants
700 North Water Street
Burnet, Texas 78611
(512) 756-7143
www.stormsrestaurants.com
Also in Lampasas, Hamilton, Marble Falls, and Kingsland, Texas

Robbis Storm told me:

"The Storm family has had a lot of experience feeding hungry travelers. The first Storm's in Texas dates back to 1873, when my great-grandfather William Washington Storm built a stagecoach stop and post office in Wood County. I'm not sure of the exact menu, but I expect my great-grandmother served up chicken fried steak and fresh catfish, much like we serve today.

"Storm's hamburgers and french fries didn't become famous until 1944, the year I was born, when my father, Jim Storm, owned and operated a diner in San Antonio. Then in 1950, my family moved back to the Hill Country to open the Dairy Cue, a name we changed twenty years later to Storm's. We're in our fifty-eighth year in that same location in Lampasas, as well as in Burnet and Hamilton. We've been around a long time and have seen many changes in the food industry. Change can be good, but in some areas we still do things the way we did fifty years ago. We're one of the few old-fashioned places that grind our own beef, so we can guarantee the flavor and quality of our famous Texas hamburgers. And for french fries we still slice fresh potatoes every day. So I invite you to try a famous Storm's hamburger or order up a plate of fresh catfish. We've been feeding folks a long time, and we're good at it.

"Here's our Chicken Fried Steak recipe from the Storm's in Burnet. Use a round steak, sized to your appetite. We generally go with half a pound or slightly less per person. I like to serve it with cream gravy, green salad, corn on the cob, and iced tea. On a cold winter day, I'd substitute mashed potatoes for the corn and double the gravy. Writing this down has made me hungry. I live about fifteen minutes from the Burnet Storm's. Think I'll run in to town and grab a chicken fried steak with gobs of gravy."

Chicken Fried Steak

1 cup all-purpose flour
½ teaspoon paprika
¼ to ½ teaspoon garlic salt
¼ teaspoon turmeric
Salt and black pepper to taste
Lawry's Seasoned Salt (optional—replaces the individual spices)
Canola oil
½ pound round steak
1 large egg
12 ounces whole milk

In a medium-size mixing bowl, combine the flour, paprika, garlic salt, salt, turmeric, and black pepper. Whisk together well. (An alternative easy way to do it at home is to use Lawry's Seasoning Salt in place of the individual spices.) Until you've done this a few times, it's better to under season. You can always add more after the steak is done.

In a large, heavy skillet over medium heat, add enough oil to cover the steaks and heat to 360°F. You do *not* want the oil to get so hot it starts smoking.

While the oil is heating, do the following. Pound the steak to flatten and tenderize it. In a medium-size mixing bowl, combine the egg and the milk and beat together well.

Use a fork or tongs to dip the steak into the egg and milk mixture, and then dredge it in the seasoned flour. For extra crust, repeat the process so you have two layers of breading.

When the oil is ready, put the steak in, being careful not splash the hot oil. How long you cook it depends on how thick the steak is. If you want it well done, wait till it floats, turn it over, and cook another minute or so. It should be an attractive golden brown when it's done.

Makes 1 serving.

Storm's Drive-In, Kingsland, Texas

14124 West FM 1431
Kingsland, TX 78639
(On Lake LBJ)
(325) 388-8899
www.stormsrestaurants.com
Also in Lampasas, Burnet, Hamilton, and Marble Falls, Texas

Earlier in the book I talked about how many modern roads have their roots in earlier pathways, like animal or Indian traces, and then later farm-to-market or stagecoach routes. Essentially a route of travel follows the lay of the land or nature, then once established is passed down from generation to generation, much like the way food traditions and recipes are inherited. It follows that one of the roots of our modern road food can be found in the meals offered to stagecoach travelers and drivers. To my great joy and surprise I was offered an original fried catfish recipe from those pioneering days from Robbis Storm. You can try it at home, and if you find yourself riding in the hill country of Texas, you can sample it from the source. Storm's has five locations, and only the Burnet and Kingsland Storm's serve this recipe. Here is what Robbis had to say:

"This fried catfish recipe is based on my great-grandmother's menu at the old stagecoach stop. The old stagecoach stop was in Wood County in East Texas. It served a stage line that ran between Mineola and Sulphur Springs. It was called 'Stormville,' and a rural community grew up around it, which included a school and least two churches. It sits on Farm to Market Road 2225 north, northeast of Quitman near the banks of Lake Fork. There's very little left there now but a place name on a map, which you can find in MAPSCO's Roads of Texas. Nowadays you can buy catfish in any supermarket. Back in the 1870s when the Storms had the stagecoach stop, they had to catch their own fish. There was no refrigeration, so any fish they served was absolutely fresh from a nearby river or creek. An interesting variant is to replace the cornmeal with cracker meal. Gives the fish a different look and a different taste. Although I personally eat my fish plain, I like to have a hot sauce like Tabasco, lemon wedges, ketchup, grated horseradish, and tartar sauce on the table for those who want it. Serve with hush puppies, green salad, french fried potatoes, and iced tea or cold beer. In the summer I like to add fresh corn on the cob."

The recipe is for one serving; since freshness is key, this allows you to adjust for the number of folks you are serving.

Storm's Great-Grandmother's Stagecoach Stop Fried Catfish

Canola oil (Great-Grandmother Storm used lard)
8 to 10 ounces fresh catfish (Great-Grandmother Storm used
    whole fish or pieces of larger fish; I prefer fillets)
1 cup stone ground white cornmeal
Salt (to taste)
Black pepper (to taste)
Red cayenne pepper (optional)

Heat the oil to 350°F in a deep pot or deep fryer.

While you're heating the oil, do the following:

Cut the fish into smaller strips, about 1.5 ounces each. The fish will cook quicker and more evenly at this size.

In a large bowl, mix the cornmeal and salt. As you add salt to the meal, taste-test it until it tastes slightly too salty. Then it's perfect, as you'll lose some of the salt during the cooking process. Then mix in black pepper to taste. If your taste buds like a little more authority, add cayenne pepper.

When the oil is up to temperature, roll the fish in the cornmeal and drop it in the oil. The moisture from the fish is enough to make the cornmeal stick (in this recipe you do not need to soak the fish in beer, lemon juice, or buttermilk before you bread it). When the pieces float, they're done, but most folks like them cooked a little longer. I usually leave them one more minute, but you should experiment to see how you like them.

Makes 1 serving.

The M*A*S*H cast enjoys a lunch of Tony Packo's hot dogs and chili provided by Tony Packo's Cafe of Toledo, Ohio. Toledo-bred actor Jamie Farr, third from left, portrayed Corporal Max Klinger on the television show. TONY PACKO'S CAFÉ

Tony Packo's—Front Street Restaurant, Toledo, Ohio

1902 Front Street
Toledo, OH 43605
(419) 691-6054
www.tonypackos.com

Chuck Johnson of Butler, Indiana, recommended Tony Packo's to me saying: "What can I say about Tony Packo's, everything is very good. Don't stop at a Tony Packo's on the edge of Toledo; go to the one downtown on Front Street, it's worth the extra drive time. Just hope you can find a place to park if you arrive at mealtime." That is dedication to a favorite restaurant's original location—Chuck would burn time and gas at today's high prices to have the original Tony Packo's at the original Front Street Restaurant.

If the name Tony Packo's sounds very familiar it should, especially if you are a fan of the classic 1970s TV hit M*A*S*H. To quote from the Tony Packo's Web site:

"The words that came out of Jamie Farr's mouth on Feb. 24, 1976 would put Tony Packo's in the spotlight. Farr, a native Toledoan himself, appeared in the television show "M*A*S*H," playing Corporal Max Klinger, a crazy medical corpsman who was also from Toledo. In the episode that made Packo's future, a man playing a television newsman talked to Klinger about his hometown. Farr wrote a little local color into his reply. The lines read, 'If you're ever in Toledo, Ohio, on the Hungarian side of town, Tony Packo's got the greatest Hungarian hot dogs. Thirty-five cents . . .' Thus a new epoch began. The name appealed to the scriptwriters, who wrote Packo's into five subsequent episodes. In one show, the mobile hospital unit asked Packo's to send sausage casings to be used in a blood-filtering machine. Packo's was also mentioned in the two-and-a-half-hour final episode in 1983."

Try this delightful Hungarian dish and you will write Tony Packo's into your next travel adventure script.

- -

Tony Packo's Paprika Chicken

2 medium-size onions, peeled and minced
2 tablespoons lard
1 plump chicken, about 3 pounds, disjointed, washed and dried
1 large ripe tomato, peeled and cut in pieces
1 heaping tablespoon "Noble Rose" paprika
½ cup water plus 1 teaspoon cold water
1 teaspoon salt
2 tablespoon sour cream
1 tablespoon flour
1 green pepper sliced
2 tablespoons heavy cream
Egg noodles

Use a 4- or 5-quart heavy casserole with a tight-fitting lid. Cook the onions in lard, covered, over low heat for about 5 minutes. They should become almost pasty, but definitely not browned. Add chicken and tomato and cook, covered, for 10 minutes.

Stir in paprika. Add ½ cup water and salt. Cook, covered, over very low heat for 30 minutes. In the beginning, the small amount of water will create a steam-cooking action. Toward the end of the 30-minute period, take off lid and let the liquid evaporate. Finally let chicken cook in its own juices and fat, taking care it does not burn. (If the chicken is tough, you may have to add a few more tablespoons of water.)

Tony Packo's Paprika Chicken, tender boneless chicken simmered in an Old World sauce, served over Hungarian dumplings TONY PACKO'S CAFÉ

▓ Remove chicken pieces. Mix sour cream, flour, and 1 teaspoon cold water, and stir with the sauce until it is very smooth and of an even color.

▓ Add green pepper, replace chicken parts, and adjust salt to taste. Put lid back on casserole and over very low heat cook until done. Just before serving, whip in the heavy cream. Serve with egg dumplings.

▓ Note: The combination of sour cream and heavy cream is the almost forgotten but ideal way to prepare this dish. Today, more often than not, the heavy cream is omitted. In Hungary, the lily is gilded by spreading several tablespoons of additional sour cream on top of the chicken in the serving platter.

Makes 4–6 servings.

Tony Packo behind the bar at Tony Packo's Café, 1902 Front Street, Toledo, Ohio, circa the 1930's—this bar is still in use today. TONY PACKO'S CAFÉ

Both the historic Lincoln Highway and the Dixie Highway passed through Toledo, Ohio. While as best I can tell, Tony Packo's is not directly on one of the old routes, it surely is one of the most famous eateries in Toledo. Here is the history of Tony Packo's from their Web site:

"The son of Hungarian immigrants, Tony Packo was a native East Toledoan. Tony was born in 1908, just a stone's throw from Consaul and Genesee streets. Tony Packo started out as a factory worker. That all changed when, in 1932, he and his wife got a $100 loan from relatives. No small feat, mind you, for this was during the hardest of hard times, the first years of the Great Depression. That same year he opened a sandwich and ice cream shop just around the corner from the place he was born. Tony had learned the restaurant business working for his older brother John, who owned a place across Consaul Street in what is now Tony Packo's parking lot. There was no beer at Packo's that first year. Prohibition would not be lifted until 1933.

"Because Tony was Hungarian-American and lived in a Hungarian neighborhood, Tony's creation was called the Hungarian hot dog. Until Toledo-born Tony invented it, there was no such thing as a Hungarian hot dog, say those who know the Old Country's food.

"Packo's food was an instant hit in the neighborhood. Within months of opening, Tony and Rose knocked out a wall and expanded their first shop, in what is now called the Consaul Tavern. By 1935, success had taken them to the point where they could buy a building of their own. They purchased the wedge-shaped establishment at Front and Consaul. The building houses part of today's Tony Packo's, but with a few more additions. The restaurant is still run by the Packo family . . . Tony and Rose's children; Tony Jr. and Nancy, and Nancy's son, Robin."

Tony Packo's Hungarian Stuffed Cabbage TONY PACKO'S CAFÉ

This stuffed cabbage recipe will surely become a favorite at your house and if it inspires you to explore one of the towns where famous highways and food cultures cross make sure to visit the Tony Packo's and tell them Biker Billy said Alright!

Tony Packo's Hungarian Stuffed Cabbage

1 head cabbage (about 3 pounds)
2 eggs
2 medium onions, finely chopped
1 clove garlic, minced
2 teaspoons salt
1¼ teaspoons paprika
⅝ teaspoon pepper
2 pounds lean ground beef (or 1 pound
    ground pork and 1 pound ground beef)

1 cup uncooked long-grain rice
1 pound sauerkraut, drained
1 (16-ounce) can tomatoes, cut up
1 (10¾ ounce) can condensed tomato soup
2 tablespoons sugar
Tony Packo's Tomato-Onion Sauce (see the
    Travel Trailer chapter)
Dairy sour cream

▨ Core the cabbage. Immerse cabbage in a 4-quart Dutch oven or kettle of boiling water and cook uncovered for about 10 minutes to wilt the leaves. Using a slotted spoon, remove the cabbage from the water; let cool slightly.

▨ Remove about 12 large leaves from the cabbage and cut out the large vein from each with a triangular cut.

▨ In a large bowl, combine the eggs, ½ cup of the onions, garlic, 1 teaspoon of the salt, 1 teaspoon of the paprika, and ½ teaspoon of the pepper. Add the meat and rice, and mix well.

▨ Place about ⅓ cup of the meat mixture on one of the 12 prepared leaves. Fold in sides. Starting at an unfolded side, carefully roll up each leaf. Repeat for the remaining leaves.

▨ Chop the remaining cabbage. In a large bowl, combine chopped cabbage, sauerkraut, undrained tomatoes, tomato soup, sugar, the remaining chopped onion, remaining 1 teaspoon salt, remaining ¼ teaspoon paprika, and remaining ⅛ teaspoon pepper.

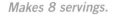 In a 6- or 8-quart heavy kettle or Dutch oven, spoon half of the sauerkraut mixture evenly in the bottom. Arrange cabbage rolls, seam side down over sauerkraut mixture. Spoon remaining sauerkraut mixture over the rolls. Fill with enough water to cover rolls.

Bring mixture to boiling. Reduce heat and simmer, covered, for about 2 hours, adding water as needed to keep rolls covered.

Meanwhile, prepare the Tomato-Onion Sauce.

To serve, transfer cabbage rolls and sauerkraut mixture to a serving bowl or platter. Spoon Tomato-Onion Sauce over cabbage rolls. Serve with sour cream.

Note: You can freeze cooked cabbage rolls for up to 6 months. To serve, let cabbage rolls partially thaw in refrigerator overnight. Place cabbage rolls in a shallow baking pan. Bake covered in a 350° oven for 35 to 40 minutes or until heated through.

Makes 8 servings.

Exterior of Tony Packo's Café, 1902 Front Street, Toledo, Ohio, located in the Hungarian neighborhood of Birmingham TONY PACKO'S CAFÉ

Appalachian Brewing Company, Gettysburg, Pennsylvania

401 Buford Avenue
Gettysburg, PA 17325
(717) 334-2200
www.abcbrew.com
Also in Camp Hill and Harrisburg, Pennsylvania

The Appalachian Brewing Company (ABC) in Gettysburg is located right on U.S. Highway 30, which was once known as the Lincoln Highway, America's first coast-to-coast route. Here is an excerpt from the ABC Web site: "ABC Gettysburg is proud to be a member of the Gettysburg community and so close to Civil War history. Located on Buford Avenue at the crest of Seminary Ridge, we're pleased to produce our trademark fine food and great beers just steps from a site so rich in local and national historical significance."

It is indeed a historic location along a most important road in America's highway history. Robin Cox, a good friend of mine and the lady who has been my culinary assistant at the Carlisle Summer Bike Fest for many years, works for ABC and recommended them to me. Knowing how good their stout is, I think you should try this stew at home.

- -

Susquehanna Stout Beef Stew

2½ pounds boneless beef chuck, trimmed of any large pieces
    of fat and cut into 1½-inch cubes
6 tablespoons (¾ stick) unsalted butter
2½ pounds yellow onions (about 5), quartered
2 pounds carrots, peeled and cut into 2-inch pieces
2½ pounds boiling potatoes, peeled and cubed
5 garlic cloves, minced
1 teaspoon salt
2 teaspoons black pepper
2 bottles Appalachian Brewing Company Susquehanna
    Stout or other suitable stout

- Preheat oven to 450°F.

- Toss all ingredients except beer into a large ovenproof casserole dish.

- Pour beer over stew, cover, and cook until the meat is very tender, the potatoes are breaking apart, and the beer is absorbed, about 2 hours.

- Remove from oven and deglaze the casserole by pouring ½ cup of water over the stew.

- Transfer stew to serving bowls and enjoy.

Makes 6 servings.

The Well-Bred Bakery & Café, Weaverville, North Carolina

26 North Main Street
Weaverville, NC 28787
(828) 645-9300
www.well-bredbakery.com

The Well-Bred Bakery & Café is located at 26 North Main Street in Weaverville, North Carolina. North Main Street is the official mailing and street address; however, like many "Main Streets" in small-town America, it has gone through lots of changes. The long-term cycle of original development, growth, decline, and rebirth has seen this Main Street have many changes and road designations. Once it was part of what was called the Old Weaverville Highway (locals still call it that sometimes), connecting Asheville with Weaverville and points north. Then it became concurrently U.S. Highway 19 and U.S. Highway 23 as parts of the numbered federal highway system. Both of those numbered highways incorporated the old Dixie Highway (a good distance north of North Carolina) with US 19 on the western division and US 23 on the eastern division.

On more current maps you will find Main Street as the concurrent pathway of Business

The Well-Bred Bakery & Café, Weaverville, North Carolina, 2008 BILL HUFNAGLE

US 19 and Business US 23. A four-lane highway had bypassed the old roads some years ago. This new four-lane is a humorous example of how getting directions from a local can be confusing yet precisely accurate due to concurrent road routings by distant road planners. The main section running north out of Asheville is simultaneously designated as U.S. Highways 19, 23, 25, and 70, and recently, future Interstate 26. Five roads as one—do taxpayers get a discount? Not likely, but I would hazard a guess that all the old highways will be bypassed (and likely resigned as "business" on their old alignments) when the new four-lane is finally upgraded to an interstate. This is a great example of how our roads have changed. Once a named local roadway, then a federal highway, then bypassed again and again. Yet along the old road the cycle of American life continues. Businesses start, grow, move, or close; families shop and kids go to school—call the road what you will, but we still use it as our local lifeline.

The Well-Bred Bakery & Café is a relative newcomer on Main Street, and they have become very popular because of both the good food and comfortable atmosphere. The Chicken Coq au Vin recipe is often featured as a "blue plate special" and served with rice pilaf and grilled squash.

Chicken Coq au Vin

4 ounces bacon, cut into ¼-inch pieces
½ pound mushrooms, cut into ¼-inch pieces
2 large onions, diced
2 carrots, peeled and sliced into ⅛-inch pieces
4 shallots, peeled and minced
2 garlic cloves, roughly chopped
2½ pounds chicken (4–6 boneless thighs)
3 cups dry sherry
¼ cup fresh parsley
⅛ cup dried marjoram
1 bay leaf
½ teaspoon dried thyme
1 teaspoon salt (a little extra to taste)
¼ teaspoon pepper (a little extra to taste)

▓ Preheat oven to 300°F.

▓ In a large skillet over medium-high heat, fry the bacon until crisp. Remove the bacon from the skillet and set aside, leaving the bacon fat in the skillet. Add the mushrooms, onions, carrots, shallots, and garlic to the skillet. Reduce the heat to medium and sauté the vegetables until browned. Drain excess fat, pour vegetables into a medium roasting pan, and set aside.

▓ In the same skillet over medium-high heat, place chicken skin-side down and season with salt and pepper. Cook until skin is browned, about 4 minutes, then flip to lightly sear the other side, about 2 minutes. Pour 1 cup of the sherry over the chicken, and then transfer the chicken and wine/juices into the roasting pan with vegetables.

▓ Add the parsley, marjoram, bay leaf, thyme, salt, pepper, and 2 cups of sherry into the roasting pan; stir with a wooden spoon to submerge. Cover and roast for 1 hour.

Makes 4–6 servings.

Bamboo Garden, Ormond Beach, Florida

749 South Nova Road
Ormond Beach, FL 32174
(386) 677-9517
www.bamboogardenormond.com

When I attend the Daytona Beach Bike Week Rally, I always make it a point to visit Bamboo Garden Restaurant. They are almost hidden in a strip mall north of Daytona Beach in the town of Ormond Beach, Florida. I first discovered them while writing an article for *Cruising Rider Magazine* humorously called "Biker Billy Eats Daytona" and have loved them ever since. After a day of riding and clowning around or doing shows, packed wall to wall with my fellow bikers, stepping into this restaurant is a quiet breath of fresh air. They have a most peaceful atmosphere and serve meals on white tablecloths, yet at modest prices. And the food is fantastic. I have taken many friends and clients here, and everyone leaves the table satisfied. Here is one of their special recipes and what owner Hanh has to say about it: "One of our favorite dishes is a Vietnamese dish called Com Tay Cam. The dish consists of pork, shrimp, chicken, and vegetables over jasmine rice served in a clay pot. It can be cooked hot, medium, or mild according to your choice."

- -

Com Tay Cam

1 teaspoon sugar
¼ teaspoon MSG (optional)
1 teaspoon oyster sauce
1 teaspoon plum sauce
2 teaspoons soy sauce
2 cups peanut oil
¼ cup sliced Spanish onion
4 large shrimp, deveined

¼ teaspoon minced garlic
½ cup sliced boiled chicken (dark meat)
½ cup sliced roast pork
8 pieces baby corn
8 pieces straw mushrooms
¼ cup peas and carrots
2 cups cooked jasmine rice

In a small bowl, combine the sugar, MSG, oyster sauce, plum sauce, and soy sauce. Stir together well and set aside.

Heat a large wok over high heat until hot, then put the oil in the wok. Add the onion and shrimp and stir-fry until shrimp is well cooked, about 2 minutes. Remove shrimp and onion from wok and set aside. Carefully drain the oil.

Return ¼ cup of the oil to the wok. Place garlic in the wok and stir-fry until it turns brown. Add the chicken, pork, baby corn, straw mushrooms, and peas and carrots to the wok and stir-fry. Cook for at least 30 seconds. Add the sauce mixture and toss well to coat. Continue to cook until the sauce has thickened.

Return the shrimp and onions to the wok and toss together well. Transfer onto a bed of jasmine rice and serve immediately.

Makes 2 servings.

When I asked Bamboo Garden owner Hanh about the restaurant's history and this dish, she told me:

"The restaurant, Bamboo Garden, has been open since 1985 and was owned by Chris Bui, my brother. Then my husband, Peter, and I took over in 1997. Our Chef Shrimp dish is a local favorite. This dish contains about thirteen large deveined shrimp coated with egg white, garlic salt, onions, Spanish onions, half teaspoon of salt, and half teaspoon of MSG. Then it is all cooked in hot oil until the shrimp turns golden brown and then poured on top of shredded lettuce."

Chef Shrimp

1 pint peanut oil
1 large egg
14 large shrimp, deveined
1½ teaspoons garlic salt
2 tablespoons cornstarch
½ cup sliced Spanish onions
½ cup green onions, cut into 2-inch-long pieces
½ teaspoon salt
½ teaspoon MSG (optional)
¼ head of iceberg lettuce, shredded

Heat the oil in a large wok over high heat to 350°F.

While the oil heats, separate the egg, reserving the white and discarding the yolk. Then place the shrimp in a medium bowl and add the garlic salt and cornstarch. Toss to coat. Pour the egg white over the shrimp and again toss well to coat.

Carefully place the shrimp one at a time into the hot oil. Fry the shrimp one at a time until golden brown, about 1 ½ to 2 minutes each. Remove and place on a paper towel. It is important to keep the oil temperature at 350°F so the shrimp are not greasy.

When all the shrimp are fried, place the Spanish and green onions into the oil and stir-fry until well cooked, about 1 minute. Then add the shrimp, salt, and MSG and stir well, cooking for about 2 minutes.

Remove mixture from the oil and drain well. Place on a bed of lettuce and serve immediately.

Makes 1 serving.

Florida Keys Scenic Highway—
Overseas Highway—U.S. Route 1

The section of U.S. Route 1 from Key Largo to Key West is often described as the road to paradise—a road that actually starts at its northernmost end in Fort Kent, Maine. US 1 is the easternmost highway in the numbered federal highway system, running about 2,000 miles from end to end. It runs close to the east coast of Florida and passes through many resort towns, including Daytona Beach, home to the famous annual motorcycle rite of spring (and now fall), Bike Week, a springtime paradise for motorcyclists.

The story of the road to paradise, like the road itself, starts far north of the Keys. In many ways it starts with a man named Henry Morrison Flagler, an American railroad tycoon. He first came to south Florida in 1878 for his first wife's health, and he stayed briefly. He returned again to Florida in 1881 with his second wife and developed a vision for Florida as a destination for out-of-state visitors. Seeing transportation as the major stumbling block to that vision, starting in 1885 he built what ultimately came to be known as the Florida East Coast Railway. By 1896 he had extended his railroad to Biscayne Bay, the site of present-day Miami. Ironically, he never felt that the area would be much more than a fishing village. In 1905, with the American construction of the Panama Canal recently under way, Flagler decided to extend his railroad to Key West, which at the time was America's closest deep-water port to the canal. The railroad extension, initially called Flagler's Folly and later known as the eighth wonder of the world (and called the Overseas Railway), was completed in 1912, about two years before the Panama Canal opened.

While Flagler saw no future in Miami, Carl Fisher saw what would become Miami Beach, then just a barrier island across the Biscayne Bay from Miami, as a fabulous location for the development of a resort city. So much so that he helped the cash-strapped owner of that barrier island, John Stiles Collins, a former farmer turned real estate developer, fund the completion of the Collins Bridge across the Biscayne Bay. Fisher received, in exchange, two hundred acres of what would become Miami Beach. The two-and-a-half-mile wooden toll bridge was the world's longest wooden bridge at the time it was completed in 1913, and it conveniently also connected with what would become the southern terminus of Carl Fisher's Dixie Highway.

In 1925, with the creation of the numbered federal highway system, the Florida part of the eastern route of the Dixie Highway would become US 1. Over the next decade the Great Depression would crush Carl Fisher's real estate dream and place the Florida East Coast Railway in financial receivership. On September 2–4, 1935, a category 5 hurricane struck parts of the Florida Keys, causing great loss of life and property damage, including severely damaging sections of the Overseas Railway. The Florida East Coast Railway, unable to afford reconstruction of the damaged sections, sold the right of way to the state of Florida.

This set the stage for the construction of the Overseas Highway; sections paralleled the Overseas Railway and also used many of the original railroad bridges. Today, although most of the roadway has been rebuilt, many original sections of the railroad roadbed and bridges still exist and are used for recreation. While a modern road, it is still predominately a two-lane highway and has for many years been the most dangerous section of highway in the state of Florida. Yet the road is the most frequently used method to reach Key West, paradise for the likes of Hemingway, President Truman's Winter White House, land of the Conch Republic, and the rainbow at the end of the highway. One road with more than one name—Florida Keys Highway–Overseas Highway–U.S. Highway 1—leads to it all.

Amish Acres, Nappanee, Indiana

1600 West Market Street
Nappanee, IN 46550
(574) 773-4188 or (800) 800-4942
www.amishacres.com

Amish Acres is located on U.S. Route 6 just west of Nappanee, Indiana. US 6 runs from its eastern terminus in Provincetown, Massachusetts, to Bishop, California, in the west. It is a part of the numbered federal highway system and is also known as the Grand Army of the Republic Highway.

Here is an excerpt from the *Amish Acres Recipes Cookbook* (Nappanee, Indiana, 2001):

"Sit down under the hand-hewn timbers of the century-old Barn Restaurant and enjoy Amish Acres' nationally famous Thresher's Dinner, a family-style feast of Amish country favorites. In tribute to the generations of Amish threshers who band together each harvest season to cut and thresh, thus separating the grain from the chaff, each other's crops in friendship and neighborliness, this feast is reminiscent of the hearty fare cooked up by the women in the wood-fired stoves, bake ovens, and smokehouses of the host farm in time for the noontime break in the threshing day. Often served out-of-doors under the shade of orchard trees, the Threshers Dinner was and remains among the best of all worlds.

"Amish Acres has been serving their Thresher's Dinner, named Indiana's Best Meal in *Home & Away Magazine,* for over three decades, and the menu has never changed. Guests choose two meats from the three that are served (country chicken, cider baked ham, and beef). The family-style meal begins with bean soup served from iron kettles and includes bowls of mashed potatoes and gravy, sage stuffing, beef and noodles, green beans, and hearth-baked bread and apple butter. Prairie-dressed waitresses return with a selection of fruit and cream pies to choose from."

Here is the recipe for their famous Thresher's Dinner, Beef.

Amish Acres' century-old barn restaurant AMISH ACRES

Thresher's Dinner, Beef

5 pounds chuck roast
3 tablespoons beef base
2 tablespoons meat tenderizer

■ Preheat oven to 300°F.

■ Cut roast into 3-inch cubes and place in a casserole dish. Add beef base and meat tenderizer. Fill with water and bake for 4 to 5 hours.

Makes 15–16 servings.

8

Vegetables and Side Dishes

Dinner or a hearty lunch at a good roadhouse, or at home, is not complete with just the entree. We have become very accustomed to being served a salad and bread to enjoy while we wait for the main course. Fancy-dancy uptown folks might expect seven courses, but we humble road travelers are happy with three: salad, main course, and finally dessert. It is a formula that works well for all-you-can-eat buffets, family-style country restaurants, and even chic urban eateries.

Consider how sad and lonely a plate would look with just some perfect crispy chicken fried steak sitting on it. Your mind and appetite would scream, "Where are the mashed potatoes and gravy? Where are the baked beans?!" Yes, to the shock and amazement of your parents, you might be overheard saying, "Where are my vegetables?"

While popular television commercials may portray folks feeding their veggies to the family dog, only to be repaid by a paw slap to the forehead, folks do like their vegetables. Sorry Madison Avenue, a serving of vegetable juice just won't cut it out here in real America. Maybe it might make an interesting change in juices for a Bloody Mary, but it won't take the place of real down-home cooked vegetables.

I have many friends who will order a salad and a vegetable plate when eating out. They are not all vegetarians, like myself. They simply like their veggies and greens. These days, some of us, as we accumulate the years and the inches around our middles, might do so out of health considerations, or maybe at the instruction of our doctors. But those things don't explain the love that goes into these recipes. Nor does it explain the growing popularity of farmers' markets or the growing trend toward organic vegetables at mainstream supermarkets.

Then there are the tremendous efforts of folks like my sweetheart, Mary, and me, who spend tons of time and hard labor on organic gardens. It comes down to the fact that although "meat and potatoes" are a staple of the American diet, we love our vegetables!

Arnold's Drive-In, Decatur, Indiana

222 North Thirteenth Street
Decatur, Indiana
(260) 728-4740

Arnold's Drive-In is located on U.S. Highway 27 in Decatur, Indiana. In 1927 this road was designated to replace what had been the western route of the Dixie Highway. Over the years the route extended from as far north as St. Ignace, Michigan, to its southern terminus in Miami, Florida. Although in some places it has been bypassed by various interstate highways, sections of it are still easily found today. Some old sections of the original route are still serving as connectors between communities bypassed by the interstates.

Here is what Arnold's owner Lori Collier had to say when she shared this recipe: "Hey Biker Billy, here is the recipe for the Bean Bake. First of all, you will need a 10-gallon kettle." Don't worry, folks, Lori has scaled the recipe down for home use, but it is so popular that even in 10-gallon batches it goes quickly at Arnold's Drive-In. She went on to tell me, "Now you have got the rooten-tootenist beans this side of the Midwest, partner! This recipe for 'Lori's Famous Bean Bake' came about by my simply 'winging it!' I wanted beans with a different kind of taste for my customers to enjoy, so I just started throwing things together! I must have done all right, cause the local newspaper food critic made the comment, 'Thumbs up to the Bean Bake! They alone are worth driving to Decatur for!'" She is 100 percent right about that!

Lori Collier's Famous Bean Bake

1 pound bacon, cut into 1-inch pieces
1 pound white onions, diced
2 (15-ounce) cans butter beans, drained and rinsed
2 (15-ounce) cans pork and beans
2 (15-ounce) cans dark red kidney beans, drained and rinsed
2 (15-ounce) cans Mexican chili beans (mild, not hot)
2 cups ketchup
2 cups brown sugar
¼ cup Liquid Smoke (very, very important to recipe!)

In a large pot, combine the bacon and onions. Sauté over high heat for 5 to 7 minutes, stirring often until crispy and almost "burnt" looking. Reduce heat to medium. Add the butter beans, pork and beans, kidney beans, and Mexican chili beans, and stir well. Add the ketchup, brown sugar, and Liquid Smoke. Blend with big paddle or spoon, and cook for about 10 minutes or until it bubbles pretty good. Turn the heat down to low and let cook for another 30 minutes.

Makes 5–6 servings.

Blue Willow Inn, Social Circle, Georgia

294 North Cherokee Road (Georgia Highway 11)
P.O. Box 465
Social Circle, GA 30025
(770) 464-2131 or (800) 552-8813
www.bluewillowinn.com

This is the recipe that made the Blue Willow Inn famous and played a part in an answered prayer. I encourage you to read the Van Dykes' cookbook, *The Blue Willow Inn Bible of Southern Cooking* (Rutledge Hill Press, 2005). You will find within its pages not only great recipes but the personal story behind how, with hard work and help from the Lord, the Van Dykes restored and preserved a historic mansion and made a dream come true. Their original headnote tells the part that this recipe played in that story:

"The Blue Willow Inn's Fried Green Tomatoes are legendary, having put the newly opened restaurant on the map shortly after a visit from famed columnist Lewis Grizzard in 1992. Following his visit, Grizzard authored a column in which he raved about the Blue Willow Inn Restaurant and the food it served, especially the Fried Green Tomatoes. Following the national publicity the restaurant received from Grizzard's column, Fried Green Tomatoes became a delicious Blue Willow tradition, and they are always served at every meal with a side of Tomato Chutney."

Blue Willow Inn's Famous Fried Green Tomatoes

3 green tomatoes
1½ cups buttermilk
2 eggs, lightly beaten
½ plus ½ teaspoon salt
½ plus ½ teaspoon black pepper
1 tablespoon plus 1½ cups self-rising flour
2 cups vegetable oil

Wash and slice the tomatoes into ¼-inch slices. In a medium-size bowl, mix the buttermilk and eggs. Add ½ teaspoon of the salt, ½ teaspoon of the pepper, and 1 tablespoon of the flour. Mix well. Place the tomato slices in the buttermilk and egg mixture. Set aside to rest.

Preheat the oil in a heavy skillet or electric fryer to 350° F. In a medium-size bowl, mix the remaining I ½ cups flour, ½ teaspoon salt, and ½ teaspoon pepper. Remove the tomato slices from the buttermilk/egg mixture and toss them, one at a time, in the flour mixture, coating them thoroughly. Carefully place the tomato slices in the heated oil and fry until golden brown. Turn them two or three times. Be careful not to crowd the tomatoes during frying. Do not allow them to overlap or stick together. Cook until crisp. Drain on paper towels. Serve immediately.

Makes 6 servings.

The next recipe is for the yummiest mashed potatoes I have ever enjoyed. They are the creation of my daughter Sarah, and by the logic of sorting recipes in this cookbook, this recipe should be in my Home Sweet Home chapter. However, they are here simply as a convenience to you, who will be looking for mashed potatoes in this chapter.

At all of our family gatherings where a special meal is the order of the day, it is Sarah, and Sarah only, who makes the mashed potatoes. We might help with the washing, peeling, and cutting chores, but once in the pot, the rule is: Step aside, mister, and let the chef work her magic. If for some reason she is not able to be with us for a celebration, we are left spudless.

Sarah shares this recipe with you and offers these tips: "It is important to use whole milk; it enhances the flavor—and the fat! You may need to use more or less salt to suit your taste buds, but this is where I like to start."

Try them at home, and I am sure you will like them.

Sarah's Yummy Taters

10 large baking potatoes
1½ cups whole milk
1 stick butter
1 cup sour cream
1 teaspoon garlic salt

1 teaspoon dried parsley
1 teaspoon paprika
1 teaspoon salt, or to taste
Dash black pepper (optional)

A yummy variation for cheese lovers:
Add 1 cup shredded cheddar cheese!

■ Wash and peel the potatoes, and cut into 1-inch chunks. Put the potatoes in a large pot and cover with water. Place over high heat and bring to a boil. Reduce the heat to medium and simmer for 20 minutes, or until tender.

■ Drain the potatoes and return to the same pot. Add the milk, butter, sour cream, garlic salt, parsley, and paprika, and mash by hand or with a hand mixer until almost smooth. Taste, and then add salt and black pepper to taste. Mix just enough to distribute the salt and pepper; the mashed potatoes should be mostly smooth but still have some small chunks. Serve hot and enjoy. Yummy, yummy!

Makes approximately 15 (1-cup) servings.

Shady Maple Smorgasbord, East Earl, Pennsylvania

129 Toddy Drive
East Earl, PA 17519
(717) 354-8222
www.shady-maple.com

My long time friend Myrrh Davis who works for BMW motorcycles recommended the Shady Maple Smorgasbord to me. As a long-distance rider and a fellow traveler along the motorcycle rally and event circuit, Myrrh has had the opportunity to sample many eateries nationwide and beyond; so her recommendation is worth listening to.

The Shady Maple Smorgasbord is located just off U.S. Route 322, a spur highway of U.S. Route 22. In Pennsylvania Route 322 is known as the "Division Highway" in honor of the 28th Division of the United State Army, the oldest division in the United States Armed Forces. The division's nickname is the "Keystone Division" and their shoulder insignia is a red keystone—the same shape as Pennsylvania uses on road signs.

These Harvard beets are both tasty and have a deep red color, much like the "Keystone Division's shoulder insignia. Enjoy them and remember to say a prayer for all our fine folks in the armed forces.

Harvard Beets

⅞ gallon beets
1 tablespoon butter, melted
1½ cups sugar
¼ cups Clear Jel
¾ teaspoon salt
¾ cup beet juice (reserve after simmering beets)
¼ cup dark vinegar

■ Place the beets in a large saucepot and cover with water, heat over high heat until the water boils, reduce the heat to low and simmer, stirring occasionally until the beets are tender. Remove from heat, drain, and reserve ¾ cup of the liquid; this will be the "beet juice." Return the beets to the saucepot and cover.

■ In a small saucepan combine the butter, sugar, Clear Jel, salt, reserved beet juice, and vinegar; cook over a medium heat until thickened. Pour the sauce mixture over the beets, gently stir until covered, and serve immediately.

Makes about a gallon.

Smoky Mountain Diner, Hot Springs, North Carolina

70 Lance Avenue
Hot Springs, NC 28743
(828) 622-7571
www.hotspringsnc.org

A fellow motorcycle enthusiast and a friend, Andy Cody, recommended the Smoky Mountain Diner to me. You will find the Smoky Mountain Diner nestled in the small mountain town of Hot Springs. The town has an interesting history both in terms of early roads and as a resort destination. In the early 1800s the Buncombe Turnpike was completed running from eastern Tennessee and Kentucky through the mountains of North Carolina and onward to the seacoast. This early road was also known locally as "The Old Drovers Road" since countless thousands market animals were "driven" to market before the railroads were built in the area. Today U.S. Routes 25 and 70 run concurrently through the middle of town and along parts of that old road; they connect Hot Springs to Asheville, North Carolina, toward the east and Kingsport, Tennessee, toward the west. Owner Genia Peterson told me:

"'The Diner,' as locals refer to the place, is a family friendly environment that offers delicious food, large portions, and a staff that can dish out a load of fun on any willing or unwilling customer. We have proudly owned the restaurant since 1993. When you visit us for the first time, you will be treated as if you were family.

"The baked bean recipe was created by the first person to cook and work at the restaurant in the early '80's when the doors opened for the first time. All the locals love to eat Robin's cooking, no matter the dish. However, her baked beans are one of her very best. Now Robin has a different job but still loves to cook for small or large armies of people frequently. We are very happy to have her baked beans every day."

The Smoky Mountain Diner is a local favorite and a yummy stop for folks visiting the area. The diner is on Lance Street, which is also State Route 209 and is located just a short distance from the juncture with U.S. Routes 25 and 70.

This recipe is a favorite at the Smoky Mountain Diner, and once you prepare it at home it will become one of your favorites. Perfect for a family picnic or as a side for any of the burger, dog, or barbecue recipes found within these pages.

Robin's Baked Beans

1 large bell pepper
1 large onion
3 pounds ground beef
1 (96-ounce) can pork-n-beans
1 quart light red kidney beans
1 (2-pound) bag of brown sugar
1 (44-ounce) bottle of ketchup
¼ cup mustard

■ **Preheat oven to 350°F.**

■ **Dice the pepper and onion. Brown the ground beef, pepper, and onion. Drain. In a large pan mix the ground beef with the remainder of the ingredients. Bake for 2 to 2½ hours, or until thick. Stir occasionally.**

Makes about 2 gallons.

The town of Hot Springs derives its name from the naturally occurring healing mineral springs in the area. Originally it was called Warm Springs for the 100°F-plus springs that had been found by Native Americans. These springs are a natural phenomenon that led to the development of a series of resorts and hotels from the late 1700s till today. Near the end of the 1800s a higher-temperature spring was discovered and the town's name changed to Hot Springs; also around those times the railroad reached the town.

It is interesting to note that the Appalachian Trail (AT) comes down from the mountain ridges and runs along the main street (U.S. Routes 25 and 70) through town. Along that common pathway the trail crosses both the railroad tracks and the French Broad River before ascending back to the mountaintops along its more than 2,100-mile course. The town of Hot Springs is both North Carolina's only Appalachian Trail town and only mineral hot springs location. As a nexus of old roads, railroads, the AT, and a river, it also forms a unique destination. On weekends one finds a colorful collection of bikers, hikers, rafters, and all sorts of folks there to enjoy the beauty of the mountains.

The Smoky Mountain Diner's location on Lance Street, which is known locally as the Appalachian Trail Highway or State Route 209, makes it easily accessible for a nourishing pause from whatever your mode of travel is. As a side note, State Route 209 is a great and sometimes challenging motorcycle road that also leads into Asheville, North Carolina.

Genia Peterson, who owns and operates the Smoky Mountain Diner shared two fabulous recipes with us. She and her team at the Smoky Mountain Diner are also known for their dedication to helping to support local charitable causes. If you are traveling through or perhaps attending the Hot Springs Motorcycle Rally, hosted by the Buncombe County Chapter of North Carolina ABATE/CBA (American Bikers Aimed Toward Education/Concerned Bikers Association), stop in and enjoy a hearty mountain meal at the Smoky Mountain Diner.

Genia told me, "Everyone is like family. We are open 365 days a year. So every Thanksgiving and Christmas only my family works at the restaurant (nothing like free labor) and my mom and I prepare this recipe to serve. We give away far more food on these days than any other. That is what we pride ourselves on, being an asset to the community while serving great food."

Sweet Potato Casserole

3 cups mashed sweet potatoes
  (pre-cooked)
1 cup sugar
½ cup melted margarine
⅓ cup milk
1 teaspoon vanilla extract

2 large eggs

Topping:
1 cup brown sugar, packed
1 cup chopped pecans
⅓ cup melted butter

▪ **Preheat oven to 350°F.**

▪ **Combine sweet potato mixture ingredients and mix well. Put in a 2-quart casserole dish. Mix topping ingredients and place on top of sweet potato mixture. Bake for 25 minutes.**

Makes 10–12 Servings.

9

Barbecue, Wings, and Chili

These three recipe subjects are probably the categories of roadhouse recipes that represent the most highly guarded secrets in the business—even more so than the secret "Coney Sauce" recipes in the Burgers and Dogs chapter. Keeping the recipes secret is based on good reasons: Barbecue, wings, and chili are very competitive genres of cuisine. There are countless competitions and contests for barbecue wings and chili on both amateur and professional levels. With barbecue, it is not uncommon for competitors to set up at least twenty-four hours in advance of the judging so they have the time to work their magic. And those folks are often outdoors, tending the fires and slow-cooking the meats in all kinds of weather. This is serious stuff to those folks, as well as seriously good eating to lots of people.

Barbecue, as the practiced high art of the many fine barbecue joints that dot the South and the heartland of America, does not lend itself to being performed in a home kitchen. Some do an admirable job with homemade or professionally built rigs in their backyards, and many a fine "Q" shack has sprung forth from those efforts. But to do a whole pig or tons of ribs and big cuts of beef or chicken by the flock, you need some serious equipment. You also need just the right kind of wood in large quantities, and the place to burn it and produce the perfect coals to slowly barbecue over. It is an art and a science with some magic tossed in.

In this chapter you will have some secret recipes revealed to you, ones that you can do at home and turn out great results. Some are award winners. So cook them at home, and if you want to pass them off as your own recipes, you might want to commit them to memory and then tear these pages out to use as kindling for your cook fire.

Doyle's Pub & Eatery, Richmond, Illinois

5604 Mill Street
Richmond, IL 60071
(815) 678-3623
www.doylespubrocks.com

I first heard about Doyle's Pub & Eatery just after I started this book project, when I received a great letter of recommendation from Robin Bertucci. Talk about getting a hot tip from a fellow rider about a great local place to eat. Here is what Robin had to say:

"How exciting, a new cookbook featuring riders' favorite road trip stops. Well, have I got a place for you. Doyle's Pub in Richmond, Illinois—this place *rocks*. Jeanne Doyle, proprietor, is herself a rider and caters to riders of all makes and models. She also prepares daily all of the homemade specialties, from soups to pastas. The Hot Wings are the best around and won the Chicago Wingfest in 2004, beating out thirty other competitors in a fierce competition. I am a wing connoisseur, and these are by far the best I've ever had, with a great, spicy sauce while remaining crispy. They're served with celery sticks and homemade blue cheese dressing (or ranch for those not so bold). Recently, Doyle's Pub won the Chili Cook-Off at Lake Shore Harley Davidson in Libertyville, Illinois. Doyle's Pub won with the most creative rendition of Bloody Mary Chili, served in a martini glass and garnished with a skewer of salami, pepperocini, onion, cheese, and an olive drizzled with Rooster Sauce. A homemade tortilla chip topped off this winning recipe.

"Doyle's Pub is a biker-friendly and family place. Every Thursday from June 'til September is Bike Night. Live music, food and drink specials, local bike builders, and vendors round out the evening. Doyle's Pub once was an operating mill, located on the Nippersink Creek on Mill Road in Richmond, Illinois, about 60 miles northwest of Chicago and just minutes from the Wisconsin border. Its quaint charm and vast collection of classic rock memorabilia make it a comfy place to visit.

"The third weekend in August, Doyle's Pub hosts Creekside Blues and Bike Fest, a three-day festival of the best Chicagoland blues bands and, of course, bikes, bikes, and more bikes, and throw in some great biker chicks, too.

"Jeanne Doyle is a very giving and generous woman, and portions of the nominal admission fee to the fest are donated to local biker charities, including I.O.O.F.–Ben Hur Lodge #870 (a national philanthropic organization) as well as BACA (Bikers Against Child Abuse) Southeastern Chapter.

"I invite your readers to stop by for a visit. Jeanne or her daughter Kierre, or bar manager Denise, will serve you up a cold draught of Guinness topped with a clover, and daughter Gracie will gladly take your food order (followed by son Quinn, who will bus your table). Sit inside, or on the deck—oh, the Reuben sandwiches are real lean and juicy, and another one of my other favorites. Hope to see you there soon! Robin Bertucci, loyal patron."

When Jeanne shared this recipe, she also shared these words of advice:

"First of all, the recipe for BBQ Wing Sauce makes just over a gallon, but it can be stored for several weeks in the fridge. I deep-fry my wings; it's the *only* way to get nice crispy skin on them. I won Best Hot Wings in Chicago's Fifth Annual Wingfest. You have to be invited to be in the contest, which was an honor in itself; but then to *win* the first time we entered—now *that* was cool!"

All I have to say, folks, is pay them a visit and tell them: Alright! Biker Billy says hello.

Jeanne and Kierre Doyle, winners of the 2007, 2nd Annual Chili Cook-Off at Lake Shore Harley Davidson in Libertyville, Illinois DOYLE'S PUB & EATERY

Doyle's Pub BBQ Wing Sauce

1 (16-ounce) can ketchup
½ cup yellow mustard
½ cup horseradish
½ cup pickle relish
Dash paprika
Dash white pepper
Dash salt

Cayenne pepper to taste
½ cup brown sugar
½ cup Worcestershire sauce
½ cup Liquid Smoke
2 cups barbecue sauce (I like Sweet
    Baby Ray's)

In a large mixing bowl, combine all ingredients and whisk together well. Let set for 1 hour. Use on naked wings or ribs.

Makes just over a gallon.

The Hearthstone Restaurant, Metamora, Indiana

18149 U.S. Highway 52
Metamora, IN 47030
(765) 647-5204

The Hearthstone Restaurant is located on U.S. Route 52 in Metamora, Indiana, a historic town that features many attractions from the canal era of American history. This section of US 52 follows the course of the Whitewater Canal, which was built between 1836 and 1847. Canals, instrumental in moving goods during the early years of the industrial revolution, were made obsolete by railroads, many of which were built using the canal towpaths as a convenient roadbed. It was only natural that roads would be built alongside the same proven pathway of transportation. US 52 is another blue line highway that, like Route 66, breaks with the tradition of being either east–west or north–south. It follows a diagonal course from Charleston, South Carolina, to Portal, North Dakota, at the Canadian border and is either bypassed or runs concurrently with several interstates along the way. When you have developed a good appetite from riding this old blue line highway and visiting the many historic attractions, head over to the Hearthstone Restaurant and try their Hot Wings and other fine foods. Here is some of the history of the Hearthstone Restaurant, as shared with me by the owners:

"Since 1930, the Hearthstone Restaurant has been renowned for country food and fine family dining. Today it is Metamora's oldest business in continuous existence.

"The Martindale family erected the original building from local materials found in the Whitewater Valley. It was then operated by the Barth and Al Brown families until 1946, when it was purchased by the Alsman family. This was the family who made the fried chicken, steak, ham, and catfish famous not only in the valley but throughout the tri-state area. In 1969, the main dining room was added, and the old dining room was converted to a lounge decorated by George C. Hillenbrand, using the theme from his horse park in Batesville.

"Simplicity, garnished with a warm welcome, good humor, and good food, was the key to success. Many of the staff have been with the Hearthstone for years, and the Alsmans' affinity for people and dedication to quality service became their legacy.

"In 1986, Tom Cruise and Dustin Hoffman enhanced the historic reputation of the Hearthstone after scenes from the Academy Award–winning *Rain Man* were shot on the premises.

"In 1991, Ruby Alsman sold the restaurant to a small group of southern Indiana men who have restaurant experience. Changes were made, including a long front porch, new banquet facilities, and additional parking. The new owners are dedicated to continuing the Hearthstone's tradition for fine family food served in a comfortable environment. Just across from the Millville locks in Metamora, Indiana."

Hearthstone Hot Wings

2 cups melted butter
10 ounces Louisiana Hot Sauce
Juice from 5 lemons
1 cup Worcestershire sauce
3 pounds fresh chicken wings

▪ In a large mixing bowl, combine the butter, Louisiana Hot Sauce, lemon juice, and Worcestershire sauce. Whisk together well. Place the chicken wings in the sauce and toss to coat. Cover and refrigerate, allowing the wings to marinate for 30 minutes.

▪ While the wings are marinating, preheat oven to 425°F.

▪ When the wings are done marinating, place them on a baking sheet, brush with sauce, and bake for 20 minutes, turning once and brushing again with the sauce. Serve immediately.

Makes 6–8 servings.

Appalachian Brewing Company, Harrisburg, Pennsylvania

50 North Cameron Street
Harrisburg, PA 17101
(717) 221-1080
www.abcbrew.com
Also in Camp Hill and Gettysburg, Pennsylvania

Many historic U.S. routes such as 11, 15, and 22 pass through Harrisburg, Pennsylvania, which is the state capital. It is also the juncture of Interstates 81, 83, and 76, making it a major travel hub for this region. From here you are a short hop from the historic high-water mark of the Confederacy, Gettysburg, Pennsylvania, and also from the Harley-Davidson plant at York, Pennsylvania. It is also the home of the Appalachian Brewing Company. Craig DiBlasi, Operations Manager, shared this recipe and told me:

"ABC is currently distributing its craft-brewed beers to restaurants and taverns in central Pennsylvania and in the greater Baltimore, Maryland, area. We established ourselves in Harrisburg, already expanded to Gettysburg and Camp Hill, and plan to open brewpubs in other locations around the mid-state as well. We plan to stay as local as possible in order to best serve our customers. Brewpub menu items include appetizers, soups, salads, sandwiches, burgers, gourmet pizzas, steaks, and seafood. ABC serves fresh innovative cuisine to match our tremendous handcrafted ales and lagers!"

Check them out next time you are in the area.

Barbeque Sauce

10 ounces Appalachian Brewing Company Susquehanna Stout, or other suitable stout

32 ounces ketchup

3 ounces cider vinegar

3 ounces Worcestershire sauce

1 ounce Texas Pete hot sauce

1 ounce Liquid Smoke

4 ounces honey

2 ounces Dijon mustard

5 ounces brown sugar, packed

2 teaspoons black pepper

2 teaspoons paprika

1 tablespoon celery seed

2 teaspoons salt

1 ounce granulated garlic

In a saucepan, heat Susquehanna Stout and reduce by 50 percent, yielding 5 fluid ounces of liquid. Remove from heat and cool. Once cooled, place remaining ingredients in a bowl and mix until well incorporated. Transfer to an airtight container labeled with the date and refrigerate. It will keep in the refrigerator for about 2 weeks.

Makes ½ gallon.

Pisgah Inn, Waynesville, North Carolina

Mile marker 408.7 of the Blue Ridge Parkway
P.O. Box 749
Waynesville, NC 28786
(828) 235-8228
www.pisgahinn.com

The Pisgah Inn, located at mile marker 408.7 of the Blue Ridge Parkway in North Carolina, is a favorite stop for local riders who enjoy riding both the parkway and the many fine roads in the Waynesville area. Besides the excellent dining room and its fine cuisine, Pisgah also has overnight accommodations. This is a very popular place for folks traveling the Blue Ridge Parkway and for weddings or special events, so advance reservations are wise.

This recipe makes four full racks of ribs and sauce to serve on the side, plenty enough to serve four hungry bikers. The rub and sauce recipes that are part of this rib recipe are very versatile and will surely find other frequent uses around your grill or kitchen. Head Chef Ian Drobka suggests: "Serve your ribs with baked beans and coleslaw and plenty of Apple Bacon BBQ Sauce."

The sauce is an integral part of the Pisgah Inn's Blue Ridge Mountain Ribs with Apple Bacon BBQ Sauce. It also makes a fine baste for use on your grill.

- -

Blue Ridge Mountain Ribs with Apple Bacon BBQ Sauce

The Blue Ridge Mountain Rub
- 3 tablespoons chili powder
- 1 tablespoon ground green peppercorns
- 3 tablespoons kosher salt
- 3 tablespoons fresh chopped garlic

▪ **In a small bowl, combine all ingredients and mix together well. Cover and refrigerate.**

Makes ½–⅔ cup of rub.

- - - - - - - - - - - - - - - - - -

Apple Bacon BBQ Sauce
   4 cups Open Pit barbecue sauce
   2 Granny Smith apples, peeled, cored and pureed
   6 pieces cooked peppered bacon, coarsely chopped
   ¼ cup light brown sugar
   1 bay leaf

   In a medium saucepan over a low heat, combine all ingredients and simmer for 30 minutes, stirring often. Remove bay leaf. Spread the warm sauce over ribs or serve it on the side.

Makes about 5 cups of sauce.

The Ribs
   3 cups pickle juice
   1 cup water
   1 cup pineapple juice
   4 racks ribs (about 5 to 6 pounds)
   The Blue Ridge Mountain Rub

   Fire up your grill, and preheat oven to 325°F.

   In a large bowl, combine the pickle juice, water, and pineapple juice. Stir well and set aside.

   Rub the ribs on both sides with the Blue Ridge Mountain Rub. Grill the ribs 3 minutes on each side, which is just long enough to sear the exterior of the ribs to brown. Remove the ribs from the grill and place in a deep baking pan. Cover the ribs with the juice mixture and bake for 3 hours. Remove the ribs from the liquid. (You can freeze the liquid and save it for your next batch of ribs.)

   Raise the oven temperature to 350°F. Coat the ribs on both sides with the sauce, place on a baking sheet, and bake for 5 minutes. Serve immediately.

Makes 4 full racks of ribs.

Blue Ridge Parkway

The parkway, as those who live near it are wont to call it, both out of familiarity by regular use and prideful affection, is a national treasure. It is the most visited site in the national park system, and interestingly it is the longest and narrowest national park in the world. Just over 469 miles long, the parkway wends its way along the peaks and ridges of the Blue Ridge Mountain range. The northern end is near Waynesboro, Virginia, and directly connects to the "Skyline Drive." The southern end is at the border of the Cherokee Indian Reservation and the Great Smoky Mountain National Park.

Construction on the Blue Ridge Parkway (BRP) began on September 11, 1935, in the Cumberland Knob area of North Carolina. The Linn Cove Viaduct around the privately owned Grandfather Mountain was the last major section, completed in September 1983. The viaduct is the most complex concrete bridge ever built and was designed to have the least possible environmental impact on the mountain. The final small sections that remained to be finished after the viaduct project were completed, and the entire length of the BRP opened on September 11, 1987, fifty-two years after the first shovelful of mountain was turned.

While a national park itself, the BRP was envisioned to be a scenic pleasure road connecting two national parks: the Shenandoah National Park in Virginia and Great Smoky Mountain National Park in Tennessee. It is a limited-access and limited-service two-lane road with a maximum speed limit of 45 miles per hour. The parkway travels through two states: Virginia and North Carolina. In traversing the mountaintops, it has twenty-six tunnels that are cut through the living stone. Only one of the tunnels is in Virginia; the other twenty-five are in North Carolina due to the ruggedness of the mountains in that state.

A journey along the BRP during spring will treat you to the many spring phases, from early to late season, in a matter of hours as you climb and descend the mountaintops. Spring arrives first at the lower elevations and later at the peaks. There is an old saying in our family that goes "spring climbs up the mountain and fall rolls back down." A journey along the parkway during the fall is spectacular as the foliage puts on quite a show, especially when seen from the many long-range mountain vistas and scenic pull-outs. Even without the vistas that are sometimes lost in the clouds and fog, the colors along the road itself are delightful. Several varieties of rhododendrons line the parkway, and from late April through June, there will be one or another in bloom at various altitudes. Of course, the peak summer season will provide you with lush greenery punctuated with wildflowers, wildlife, and lots of fellow travelers enjoying this tranquil escape from overdeveloped highways. So if you travel this road, take it for what it was meant to be: a slow-paced scenic pleasure ride.

Pack a picnic lunch, or leave the parkway to sample some of the places that shared their recipes.

The Buck Tavern, Corbin City, New Jersey

621 Route 50
Corbin City, NJ 08270
(609) 628-3117
www.bucktavern.com

I had the wonderful opportunity to entertain some of our wounded warriors with the American Postal Workers Union (APWU) during Rolling Thunder XX on Memorial Day weekend 2007. It was an honor to meet the fine young men and women who have served our nation so proudly. It was an experience I will never forget, and I will forever be thankful for their service and sacrifices. God bless them one and all!

During the event I worked closely with Sue Carney, National Human Relations Director for the APWU. When Sue heard about this book she sent the word out to her membership. You have to know that folks who work at your local post office have a pulse on what goes on in their town, and therefore where to find the real good local food. I would say that a restaurant recommendation from your letter carriers or post office clerks is right up there with one from a motor cop. If you ever see a bunch of police bikes outside a restaurant (no flashing lights), you know the food is good. Imagine all day riding a bike—you better be eating good food.

Dawn Formica, a South Jersey–area local APWU member, recommended the Buck Tavern by saying, "Rustic, cozy, and warm, the Buck Tavern has been a favorite rendezvous for hunters and a favorite stop for shore travelers for over sixty years. Features hearty fare and shore point staples, but it's their hot wings with Buck sauce (a special blend of blue cheese and hot sauce) that is a tavern favorite."

When I asked owner and chef Rob Ohlsen for the recipe, he was happy to share it and told me, "The Buck Tavern is located on a country road in Corbin City, New Jersey. Its rustic, warm cabin-like atmosphere embraces you from the moment you walk in. The variety of menu choices from steaks to pasta and prime rib are all proven winners. But what shines the most are the 'Famous Buck Wings' I created fourteen years ago—these crispy diamonds are a true find and a must-try for locals and travelers."

He also shared with me: "Besides being the owner-operator of the Buck Tavern, I am a graduate of the Culinary Institute of America and the founder of the American Culinary Federation Epicurean Society of Southern New Jersey."

Buck Wings

6 to 8 ounces all-purpose flour for coating
4 ounces wing seasoning (you can purchase this at your local grocery store in the spice aisle)
Salt and pepper to taste
10 fresh jumbo wings
3 ounces Crystal hot sauce
2 ounces chunky blue cheese dressing
Celery sticks for dipping

Preheat a deep fat fryer to 375°F.

In a small bowl, combine the flour, wing seasoning, and salt and pepper. Whisk together well.

Lightly dredge the wings in the seasoned flour and deep-fat–fry until crispy and completely cooked, about 4 to 6 minutes or until golden brown and crispy. Do not crowd the wings in the fryer as this will lower the temperature and may make them greasy.

In a small bowl, combine the hot sauce and blue cheese dressing and mix well. Place the cooked wings in the sauce combo and toss to thoroughly and evenly coat, making sure both the sauce and the dressing are evenly distributed. You can adjust the degree of hotness based on altering the ratio of hot sauce to blue cheese. Serve with celery sticks, which are for garnish and dipping in the extra sauce. Eat and enjoy!

Makes 1–2 servings.

Biker Billy and his 1996 Harley-Davison FLHP-I Road King Police Bike SARAH K. NIX

Deal's Gap Motorcycle Resort, Tapoco, North Carolina

17548 Tapoco Road
Tapoco, NC 28771
(800) 889-5550 (United States and Canada only) or (828) 498-2231 (outside United States)
www.dealsgap.com

Deal's Gap Motorcycle Resort is located at the eastern end of the Dragon. For those of you who have been out of circulation for too long, the Dragon is the most famous 11 miles of pavement in the world. Packed into that short stretch of asphalt are 318 turns. This adrenaline-pumping road is also known as U.S. Route 129. It travels from Tennessee to North Carolina along the southern end of the Great Smoky Mountain National Park.

About this chili restaurant manager, Jessica Venable said, "You have your choice of using jalapeños or habañeros depending on how much fire you want." Around Biker Billy's kitchen, both would end up in the chili. Jessica also shared her family recipe for Deal's Gap Slayer Corn Bread (see the Travel Trailer chapter) and told me: "This is the only corn bread my family will eat anymore, and it is a must with this fiery chili!" Try both of these recipes at home, and you will surely be well fueled and fired-up enough to ride out in search of dragons to slay.

Dragon Breath Chili

3 pounds ground beef (chuck or round)
2 medium or large onions, chopped
1 large green pepper, chopped
3 (28-ounce) cans diced tomatoes
2 (28-ounce) cans light red kidney beans
1½ tablespoons garlic powder, or more to taste
1 (3- to 4-ounce) container chili powder
Salt and pepper to taste
1 (14- or 15-ounce) can tomato paste
2 to 4 jalapeño peppers, finely chopped
2 to 4 habeñero peppers, finely chopped (optional)
Deal's Gap Slayer Corn Bread (see the Travel Trailer chapter)

In a large frying pan over medium heat, brown the ground beef; drain off excess grease and discard. Remove the beef from the pan and set aside. In the same frying pan over medium heat, sauté the onions and green peppers until tender. In a large stockpot combine the beef, onions, green peppers, diced tomatoes, and beans and bring to a boil.

Reduce the heat to low and add garlic powder, half of the chili powder, and salt and pepper. Stir well and let simmer about 30 minutes. Add the tomato paste and the jalapeño and habañero peppers. Stir well and cook another 60 minutes or longer, stirring occasionally. The longer it simmers, the better the flavor. Serve with Deal's Gap Slayer Corn Bread.

Makes about 15 servings.

Moose Café, Asheville, North Carolina

570 Brevard Road
Asheville, NC 28806
(828) 255-0920

Located right next to the Western North Carolina Farmers Market on Brevard Road, which is also known as North Carolina Route 191, the Moose Café is a must-visit place to get a taste of the mountains. If you are traveling on the Blue Ridge Parkway, exit at mile marker 393, which is also the location of the North Carolina Arboretum. At the traffic light at the bottom of the ramp, turn left onto NC 191 North. You will pass some shopping centers and cross over Interstate 26; in just another mile or two you will see the Moose Café and the Western North Carolina Farmers Market on the right, just before the ramp for Interstate 40 eastbound. They are located very conveniently just south of Asheville, North Carolina. Have a hearty meal of this chili, and you will be ready to walk it off at the arboretum or at the nearby Biltmore House.

- -

Homemade Moose Chili

3 pounds ground beef
1 onion, coarsely chopped
2 green peppers, cored and diced
2 (16-ounce) cans kidney beans, drained
2 (16-ounce) cans diced tomatoes
1 (32-ounce) bottle ketchup
4 tablespoons chili powder
1 tablespoon Worcestershire sauce
1 teaspoon ground cumin
2 cups water
Salt and pepper to taste
Chopped onions
Shredded cheddar cheese
Sour cream
Corn bread

In a large sauté pan over medium heat, combine the beef, onion, and green peppers. Sauté for 10 to 15 minutes until the beef is completely cooked and no longer has any pink color. Remove from heat and drain off fat. Add the beans, tomatoes, ketchup, chili powder, Worcestershire sauce, cumin, water, and salt and pepper. Bring to boil, reduce the heat to low, and simmer for 30 minutes or until thickened and turned a deep red. Serve with chopped onions, shredded cheddar cheese, sour cream, and corn bread.

Makes 8–12 servings.

Mrs. Rowe's Restaurant and Bakery, Staunton, Virginia

74 Rowe Road
Staunton, VA 24401
(540) 886-1833
www.mrsrowes.com

Like so many of the true jewels of American road food culture, Mrs. Rowe's Restaurant and Bakery grew up along a road that became part of the numbered road system created by the Federal Highway Act of 1921. Fortunately her place survived the construction of the interstate highway system created by the Federal-Aid Highway Act of 1956, saving this part of history for generations to come. Mollie Bryan, author of *Mrs. Rowe's Restaurant Cookbook: A Lifetime of Recipes from the Shenandoah Valley,* shared this part of the Mrs. Rowe's story with me:

"Since 1947, Mrs. Rowe's Restaurant and Bakery, Staunton, Virginia, has been welcoming travelers with down-home dishes like meat loaf, spoon bread, macaroni and cheese, and coconut cream pie. The restaurant is also so endearing to the locals that it was saved in the 1960s when Interstate 81 came through; when officials designed it they made sure the highway did not destroy this little piece of culinary heaven. Instead, it has flourished and is now one of the most successful family-owned restaurants in the state of Virginia."

Mollie also told me, "This recipe was found tucked away in one of the Rowe family's recipe notebooks on crumbly, yellowed paper." Think about that next time you decide to clear out some old boxes of family stuff—there might be a jewel of a recipe tucked away in an old book. Watch for them; they are a part of your family history, after all.

Mrs. Rowe's Chili

1½ pounds ground beef
2 green bell peppers, cored and finely chopped
1 medium onion, finely chopped
3 celery stalks, finely chopped
1 teaspoon salt
½ teaspoon ground white pepper
3 tablespoons chili powder
1½ teaspoons garlic powder
1 tablespoon sweet paprika
2 teaspoons beef base
2 cups ketchup

■ Brown the ground beef in a large pot over medium-high heat. Drain off any grease. Stir in the bell peppers, onion, and celery and cook until the vegetables soften, about 8 minutes.

■ Stir in the salt, white pepper, chili powder, garlic powder, paprika, and beef base. Cook, stirring occasionally, for 10 minutes.

■ Stir in the ketchup and continue to cook until the chili thickens, about 10 minutes. Serve at once or cool.

Makes about 2 quarts.

Top of the Hill Grill, Brattleboro, Vermont

632 Putney Road
Brattleboro, VT 05301
(802) 258-9178
www.topofthehillgrill.com

While it is almost impossible to get a great barbeque place to share their secret Pulled Pork recipe, my friend Jon Julian from Top of the Hill Grill in Brattleboro, Vermont, shared his. Jon spent a long time touring and study great barbeque in the South to learn his art and then adapt it to please the finicky New England palette of his customers.

Here is what Jon told me when he shared this secret recipe:

"I needed to experiment a bit to make sure this would work on a much smaller scale than what I do at the Top of the Hill Grill. I doubt that your readers would want to make 150 lbs of pork at one time.

"I adhere to the 'slow and low' school of BBQ. That is low cooking temperatures for a long period of time. Without going into the science behind it, this method was traditionally used to tenderize tough, inexpensive cuts of meats. I use a bone-in Boston Butt, trimmed, with about ¼-inch fat cap. This fat keeps the meat moist during its time in the cooker and I believe that the bone adds to the flavor. At my restaurant, I have commercial smokers. I set them at night, go home, and the goods are done the next morning. For those at home, I think that the following method, while still taking a lot of time, will deliver an excellent product. It utilizes a charcoal grill as well as the oven. You will need a dry spice mixture to rub into the Boston Butt. I make my own, but there are many others that are commercially available."

Jon also shared his "Top of the Hill Grill Dry Rub" recipe, which you will find in the Travel Trailer chapter.

Top of the Hill Grill Pulled Pork

1 (6- to 8-pound) Boston butt, bone-in, trimmed, with about ¼-inch fat cap
Top of the Hill Grill Dry Rub or commercial dry rub mixture (for the Hill Grill recipe, see the
    Travel Trailer chapter)
½ cup cider vinegar
Barbeque sauce

▨ Rub a Boston butt with a dry spice mixture. I make my own, but there are many others that are commercially available.

▨ Wrap butt in aluminum foil and let it be a few hours or overnight in the fridge. Bring up to room temperature prior to cooking.

▨ Light a charcoal grill. I only use a natural hardwood charcoal.

▨ Push coals to one side of the grill, mounding slightly.

▨ Place a foil-wrapped packet of pre soaked hardwood chunks (e. g., hickory), on top of the mounded charcoal. Poke a few small holes in the packet to allow smoke to escape.

▨ Place unwrapped butt in a disposable aluminum pan. The pan should be placed opposite the mounded charcoal.

▨ Add a few pieces of charcoal every 45 minutes or so, trying to maintain a 250°F, smoky environment. Avoid the temptation of constantly removing the lid. I put a thermometer in the lid vent hole and more or less was able to check the temp. Cook for 3 hours.

▨ Preheat oven to 300°F.

▨ Remove pan from grill and tightly wrap with heavy aluminum foil.

▨ Place pan in a 300°F oven and roast until fork tender, about another 2½ hours.

Let butt rest for 45 minutes. Keep it wrapped.

When cool enough to handle, pull bone (it should easily come out), and remove all the visible fat. The meat should be succulent, juicy, and smoky. "Pull" it into thin shreds. I sprinkle it with cider vinegar and then toss it with my own BBQ sauce. This is where regional variations come into play. Some people like to go in a "mustard" direction, others use a vinegar-based spicy sauce. I use a New England–style, ketchup-based sauce, which seems to work well for the Northern palette as it is not too spicy.

Note: This recipe will also work on a gas grill. Place wood chips in an aluminum pan over the primary burner, leaving the other burners off or on low. Again, try to maintain a smoky, 250°F environment. Proceed as directed with the oven steps.

Makes 6–12 servings.

SARAH K. NIX

10

Desserts

What would road food be without a hot cup of Joe and a warm slice of homemade apple pie cozied up with a scoop of vanilla ice cream? Unfulfilling, that's what! You might pass on dessert at home in a vain attempt to "watch your diet." But who does that on vacation? For that matter, when far off from the comforts of home, who really doesn't enjoy the comforts of dessert?

Is it any wonder that many diners have great chrome and glass display cases filled with luscious pies and cakes right at the entrance to the dining room? Or consider those little advertising placards left on the tables with gorgeous photos of sinfully rich desserts. Yes, every restaurateur worth his or her salt knows you crave dessert.

Road-tripping is always an adventure. Some days it is fraught with challenges, while others pass so easily they seem almost routine except for the ever-changing scenery. Whether you are finishing a day so full of challenges that it will make an epic story to be told time and again, or it was a clockwork-smooth day, you will surely feel you deserve a nice dessert. Some days the best road trip story is the dessert you found at some little eatery.

I believe it was Ernestine Ulmer who first said, "Life is uncertain. Eat dessert first." Good advice if you ask me. With that advice in mind I offer to you the recipes in this chapter, all worthy of being the adventure of the day—desserts to tell stories about. So grab a napkin and a fork or a spoon and dig in.

Stacks of yummy cookies at The Well-Bred Bakery & Café, Weaverville, North Carolina BILL HUFNAGLE

Amish Acres Shoofly Pie   AMISH ACRES

McKittrick Hotel Penny Bar and Café, McKittrick, California

23273 Highway 33
McKittrick, CA 93251
(661) 762-7676

Mike and Annie Moore own and operate the McKittrick Hotel Penny Bar and Café. Here is their story as told by Annie:

"On Friday, Saturday, and Sunday mornings it is a tradition at the McKittrick Hotel Penny Bar and Café to give a sample of whatever sweet treat or coffee cake Annie bakes to customers to enjoy while they wait for their breakfast to be served. This 'Hawaiian Delite' recipe is the Friday favorite.

"Mike and Annie dreamed of owning a bar and cafe for many years. The plan to cover the bar with pennies was also part of their dream. While Annie collected pennies, Mike didn't fully understand her dream. After finding and buying the McKittrick hotel (which is not an operating hotel, but a bar and cafe in an old historic hotel building), Mike covered the bar top with pennies and was quite proud of his accomplishment. Until Annie asked, 'When are you going to finish the bar?' He replied, 'The whole bar?' Six years later, the bar was covered with pennies. Walls, floors (the floor was covered only after Annie bribed Mike with a new Harley-Davidson motorcycle), bar kick plate, back wall, whiskey shelves, pool table, and even an old television set, which is used as a display. The bar is beer and wine only.

"Mike and Annie's McKittrick Hotel Penny Bar and Café is now world famous due to the over one million pennies Mike has attached to everything. The pennies caught the attention of the media and have been included in many magazines, on TV, and on talk radio shows. Mike and Annie and the penny bar were featured on the *Today Show* on Mother's Day in 2007. It is a fun place to stop on Highway 33 in McKittrick, California, which is a favorite back road for bikers and tourists alike. Throughout the week, oilfield workers and power plant employees mostly support the business; all of our customers are good people and greatly appreciated."

Hawaiian Delite

The Cake
   Nonstick cooking spray
   1 (18½-ounce) box yellow cake mix
   4 large eggs
   ⅓ cup vegetable oil
   1 (15-ounce) can mandarin oranges, with juice

The Frosting
   1 (20-ounce) can pineapple chunks, with juice
   1 (3.4-ounce) package instant vanilla pudding
   ½ teaspoon almond extract
   1½ cups Cool Whip
   1½ cups flaked coconut

▨ Preheat the oven to 350°F and grease a 9x13x2-inch baking pan with nonstick cooking spray.

▨ In a mixer combine the cake mix, eggs, oil, and oranges, and blend on low speed for 30 seconds. Then beat at medium speed for 2 minutes. Pour the cake batter into the greased pan and bake for approximately 45 minutes. Insert a toothpick in the center of the cake; if it comes out clean, the cake is done. Remove from the oven and let cool.

▨ In a mixer break down the pineapple chunks by mixing on low (watch for flying chunks). (Crushed pineapple can be used, but I prefer the larger chunks in the frosting.) Add the instant pudding and the almond extract and mix for about 2 minutes. Blend the Cool Whip into this mixture by folding in with a rubber spatula. Frost the cooled cake and sprinkle with coconut. Enjoy!

Makes 20 sample-size servings.

- -

The Hop Ice Cream Shop, Asheville, North Carolina

640 Merrimon Avenue
Asheville, NC 28804
(828) 254-2224

Every experienced traveler knows that warm apple pie cozied up to vanilla ice cream is the classic roadside desert. There truly is nothing better than when you can get the combination of fresh homemade apple pie and homemade ice cream—just like they made them back in the old days before desserts were manufactured in a factory and delivered by a food service company. Well, this yummy apple pie is the real deal and makes the perfect companion for the incredibly fresh ice cream that has made the Hop famous in Asheville, North Carolina. Fame well deserved for both the fresh quality and flavor selection of their ice creams, which are all made on site. Beyond making sinful real-cream ice cream, they are also known for their vegan soy milk and nut milk (cashew and almond) creations. They even make some sugar-free

The Hop's original location in a converted 1954 vintage service station ASHLEY GARRISON

varieties, so something sweet for everyone can be found here. When asked what type of apples she uses for this pie, the owner, Ashley Garrison said, "I like to use a variety of apples, like Braeburn, Granny Smith, and Gala." For those of you who don't know, Asheville is located in the renowned apple-growing region of western North Carolina.

Until recently the Hop was located in a classic gas station building that dates from 1954, with the service bay converted to a drive-through. They have since outgrown that very small building and moved to a strip mall a half mile up Merrimon Avenue, which is also known as old U.S. Route 25, which along with several other U.S. routes has been locally bypassed by Interstate 26.

Ashley Garrison's Homemade Apple Pie

Crust
2 cups all-purpose flour
½ teaspoon salt
1 teaspoon sugar
½ cup shortening
½ cup cold unsalted butter
½ cup cold water

Filling
5 to 6 cups apples, peeled, cored, and thinly sliced
1 cup sugar
¼ cup flour
1 teaspoon ground cinnamon
¼ teaspoon ground nutmeg
¼ teaspoon salt
2 tablespoons unsalted butter, softened

Egg wash
1 egg white
1 tablespoon water
1 teaspoon sugar

To make the dough for the crust, combine the flour, salt, and sugar in large bowl and mix well. Using a pastry blender or two knives crisscrossed, cut in the shortening and butter until a pea-size meal is created. Sprinkle in the cold water and mix with a fork until a dough begins to form. Form the dough into two equal balls, wrap tightly with plastic wrap, and refrigerate for 20 minutes.

Preheat the oven to 400°F.

To make the filling, combine the apples, sugar, flour, cinnamon, nutmeg, and salt in a large bowl. Toss well to mix and completely coat all the apples. Cover and set aside while you prepare the crust.

To make the crust, roll out one dough ball on a floured surface with a floured roller to form a 14-inch circle. Carefully line a 10-inch pie dish with the circle of dough and fold the edges under. Roll out the second crust into a 12-inch circle and set aside. Pour the apple filling into the piecrust, and then dot with small pieces of the butter. Carefully cover the filled pie with the second crust, fold the extra dough under the edges, and pinch flute to seal.

To make the egg wash, combine the egg white and water in a small bowl and whisk together. Brush the top of the piecrust lightly with the egg wash and sprinkle with the sugar. Cut slits in the top crust to vent. Bake for about 50 minutes or until the thickened juices bubble through the slit and the crust is golden brown.

Makes 1 (10-inch) pie.

Inside The Hop's new location, where they now offer gourmet coffees, desserts, plus an expanding menu ASHLEY GARRISON

The Hop is a locally famous ice cream parlor in Asheville, a beautiful city nestled in the Blue Ridge Mountains of North Carolina. Many roads cross through this scenic area, the most famous of which is the Blue Ridge Parkway, which scribes a graceful arc along the ridgetops east of town. The Biltmore Estate, America's largest home, is just one among many interesting sights to be found here. Another more modest dwelling, yet equally famous, is the Thomas Wolfe House, which he immortalized in his twentieth-century classic novel, *Look Homeward, Angel.*

Once you have worked up a powerful thirst touring those two historic Southern homes, I would recommend a visit to the Hop, where this java-enhanced shake will recharge your mind while cooling your weary body. Being a tourist does burn off a lot of calories, right?

The Hop's Hot-Rod Mocha Java Milkshake

1 pint (3–4 scoops) premium vanilla ice cream
¼ cup strong brewed coffee or espresso (chilled)
1 to 2 ounces Hershey's chocolate syrup
½ cup 2 percent milk or whole milk
Whipped cream

▨ Combine the ice cream, coffee, chocolate syrup, and milk in a blender and mix until smooth. (If the shake is too thin, add more ice cream; if it's too thick, add more milk.)

▨ Pour into a large chilled glass, garnish with whipped cream, and enjoy!

Makes 1 serving.

The Well-Bred Bakery & Café, Weaverville, North Carolina

26 North Main Street
Weaverville, NC 28787
(828) 645-9300
www.well-bredbakery.com

The Well-Bred Bakery & Café is one of sweetheart Mary's and my favorite places to start a Sunday's ride and adventure. They are located in what had once been the town drugstore and have on their walls some pictures of the old soda counter and the interiors and exteriors of that business. The drugstore has since moved down the main street to a new building. They are part of a rebirth of downtown Weaverville, and I find them to be a great example of the renaissance that is happening all along America's old roads, also called "blue line highways." I believe we all to some extent seek those halcyon days of old, when times were simpler and slower paced. The era of open-top touring cars has returned with the ever-more popular modern convertibles, and it takes but a quick glance across the floor of a Harley-Davidson dealership to see the retro styles.

So at the Well-Bred Bakery & Café, we can step back in time, or more accurately, into the future, and enjoy food and camaraderie at a pace that suits our souls.

Pumpkin Cheesecake

2 cups ginger molasses cookies,
    ground into crumbs
1½ pounds cream cheese
1½ cups sugar
1 tablespoon cornstarch
5 large eggs

3 tablespoons vanilla extract
1½ cups canned pureed pumpkin
1¼ cups sour cream
2 teaspoons ground cinnamon
½ teaspoon ground nutmeg
½ teaspoon ground cloves

Preheat oven to 350°F.

To prepare the crust, press the cookie crumbs into the bottom of a 9-inch springform pan. Place inside a larger pan and fill outer pan halfway with hot water. Set aside.

To prepare the filling, in a large mixing bowl mix together the cream cheese and sugar until the texture is smooth and creamy. While continuing to mix, add in the cornstarch, eggs, vanilla, pumpkin, sour cream, cinnamon, nutmeg, and cloves. Mix for several minutes until well blended.

Transfer the filling mix into the prepared pans and bake for 1 hour. The center should still jiggle slightly. Turn oven off, but keep in oven for at least 30 minutes. Refrigerate overnight.

Makes 1 cheesecake.

The tempting dessert case at The Well-Bred Bakery & Café, Weaverville, North Carolina BILL HUFNAGLE

The Filling Station, Lexington, Illinois

905½ West Main Street
Lexington, IL 61753
(309) 365-8813

If you are traveling along the stretch of old U.S. Route 66 south from Chicago, you will pass through the town of Lexington. Head into town, and you will find the Filling Station. Park your wheels and let your motor cool while you go inside to sample this mouthwatering pie. Have a cup of their great java, and when you take that first bite of pie, close your eyes and listen—you may just hear the ghosts of Packards, flathead Fords, or the *potato-potato* sound of a vintage Knucklehead Harley cruising the 66 of legends. Just remember, don't keep your eyes closed too long, or your riding buddies might just eat your pie while you are napping.

Coconut Meringue Pie

Coconut Filling
¾ cup sugar
½ cup Pillsbury's Best All-Purpose or Unbleached Flour
¼ teaspoon salt
2¼ cups milk
3 eggs, separated
3 tablespoons margarine or butter
1½ teaspoons vanilla
1 cup shredded sweetened coconut
1 (9-inch) prepared flaky piecrust

In a medium saucepan, combine the sugar, flour, and salt. In a medium bowl, beat milk and egg yolks until smooth, and then stir into sugar mixture. (Reserve egg whites for meringue.)

Cook over medium heat until mixture thickens and boils, stirring constantly, then boil slowly for 1 minute, stirring constantly. (Use care not to scorch the mixture; if you have a double boiler, using it will make it easier to do with out scorching.) Remove from heat; stir in margarine and vanilla. Add coconut and stir well, and then pour into the prepared piecrust. Allow to cool to room temperature.

Meringue
3 egg whites
⅛ teaspoon salt
¼ teaspoon cream of tartar
½ cup sugar
½ cup shredded sweetened coconut

Preheat oven to 350°F.

In a medium bowl, combine the reserved egg whites, salt, and cream of tartar and beat with mixer until stiff. Add sugar and beat until stiff peaks form.

To assemble the pie, spoon the meringue on top of the pie and sprinkle with the coconut. Bake until golden brown, about 7–10 minutes or less.

Makes 1 (9-inch) pie.

Route 66: The Mother Road

Route 66 is, in many ways, the ultimate highway of American folklore and legend. Storied from popular songs to television shows, from books to movies, Route 66 is woven into the very soul of the American road and motor culture. We have all heard Bobby Troup's "Get Your Kicks On Route 66," which was composed in 1946 and first recorded by Nat King Cole. You probably have seen reruns of the CBS television show *Route 66,* which originally aired from 1960 to 1964. The journey of the Joads in Steinbeck's classic novel *The Grapes of Wrath* and the 1940 John Ford movie based on the novel and starring Henry Fonda seem perfectly set on the Mother Road. Even the animated 2006 Pixar hit movie *Cars* taps the cultural well of this iconic road.

U.S. Highway 66 was born of several forces. Officially designated on November 11, 1926, it was part of the new numbered system of federal highways. The route leads from Chicago to Los Angeles, and unlike most U.S. highways, it is not a north–south or east–west road, rather cutting a diagonal course. The route's origins can be traced back to well before motor vehicles to an 1857 War Department wagon road. It assumed parts of several of the named roads that had developed in the preceding decade, including a good portion of the National Old Trails Road, which was a major ocean-to-ocean competitor with the Lincoln Highway.

Another force in the highway's creation was Cyrus Avery, the man probably most responsible for the birth of Route 66, who served on the federal board that created the federal highway system in 1925. He went on to promote the road and the creation of the U.S. Highway 66 Association, earning the moniker "Father of Route 66." It is interesting to note that Cyrus Avery was greatly involved with the early "Good Roads Movement." He served as an elected or appointed official in both government and private highway commissions and associations.

Route 66 served America well by helping to develop the many communities and businesses along it, providing a migration route from the dust bowl of the 1930s. In the 1940s, it carried World War II support traffic and migration, and it served as a vacation and pleasure road during the 1950s through the 1960s. It, like other blue line highways, became a victim of the 1956 Interstate Highway Act and was incrementally bypassed over the years until it was officially decommissioned in 1985.

The most commonly accepted cultural lore tells us the concept of "buildings as advertising billboards" was developed along Route 66. While this has merit, it was not an exclusive phenomenon. This, like all trends in the development of the American road and the businesses that flourished along them, was mirrored in many communities on their local highways. But there are some firsts that happened on the Mother Road. The first drive-through eatery was opened in 1947 in Springfield, Missouri, by Sheldon "Red" Chaney. The sign out front read, RED'S GIANT HAMBURG; he measured the sign and letter sizes incorrectly and didn't have room for the "ers" of *hamburgers*. Red's, like the road that it served, was immortalized in the Morells song "Reds" on their *Shake and Push* album, released by Borrowed Records in 1982. While you might find the vintage vinyl or the song on the Internet, Red's Giant Hamburg was torn down in 1997.

Another first that has lasted much longer is McDonald's. Their first location was on Route 66 in San Bernardino, California. But the bulldozer of change never rests. The original McDonald's building is gone, and the 1953 classic "Golden Arches" building that replaced it on that site is also gone. Today the site houses the "Unofficial McDonald's Museum" opened on December 12, 1998, which was the fiftieth anniversary of the original's opening.

While many buildings and landmarks are disappearing, the Mother Road is not gone. It is experiencing a growing revival and is supported by associations and individuals across America and the world. Every year, thousands of people make pilgrimages to ride on the remaining parts of the original road and on the many realignment sections that were paved over the years.

Blue Willow Inn, Social Circle, Georgia

294 North Cherokee Road (Georgia Highway 11)
P.O. Box 465
Social Circle, GA 30025
(770) 464-2131 or (800) 552-8813
www.bluewillowinn.com

Here is one of my all-time favorite Southern desserts. No matter where I travel and find a meal along the highways and byways of this great country, if there is peach cobbler available, I always am interested. If it happens to be on the buffet, I will always try it. I guess it has something to do with childhood memories. This dessert comforts my soul. I guess I am not alone in this feeling, as evidenced by the original headnote that Louis and Billie Van Dyke included in their book, *The Blue Willow Inn Bible of Southern Cooking* (Rutledge Hill Press, 2005), which follows.

"No meal at the Blue Willow Inn is complete without 'a little taste' of peach cobbler. No matter what other desserts may be arrayed in the center of the buffet room, it is ever-present on the side, where bowls of it can supplement any other end-of-the-meal sweet."

Blue Willow Peach Cobbler

¾ cup plus 2 tablespoons granulated sugar
1 cup self-rising flour
¼ cup plus ¼ cup (1 stick) butter, melted
1 (28-ounce) can undrained sliced peaches

Preheat the oven to 350°F.

In a medium-size mixing bowl, coarsely mix together ¾ cup of the sugar, the flour, and ¼ cup of the melted butter. Sprinkle about one-third of this mixture on the bottom of a baking dish. Add the peaches and juice. (If the juice does not cover the peaches, add a small amount of water just to cover the peaches. Too little liquid will make the cobbler dry. Too much liquid will make it soupy.) Top the peaches with the remaining sugar/flour mixture. Sprinkle the top with the remaining 2 tablespoons of sugar and the remaining ¼ cup of butter. Bake for 30–40 minutes or until brown and bubbly. Serve hot.

Hint: Fresh peaches can be used. When using fresh peaches, peel and slice them, sprinkling the slices with an additional ½ cup sugar. Refrigerate them for 2 to 3 hours before using.

Makes 6–8 servings.

Moose Café, Asheville, North Carolina

570 Brevard Road
Asheville, NC 28806
(828) 255-0920

Here is a sinfully delish dessert that they serve at the Moose Café. Their dishes are made from fresh seasonal goodies from the Western North Carolina Farmers Market next door. If you have room after one of the hearty mountain-fresh meals they serve, order this pie. The combination of chocolate, Oreos, ice cream, Kahlúa, and nuts will satisfy any road warrior's sweet tooth. Then head next door to the farmers' market and walk it off while you score some mountain treats to bring home to friends and family. You'll find everything from mountain ham or jams to chowchow or pickled watermelon rind, and all sorts of seasonally fresh produce.

Colorado River Mud Pie

3 ounces unsweetened baking chocolate
2 tablespoons butter or margarine
1 cup sugar
½ teaspoon salt
1½ cups evaporated milk
½ teaspoon vanilla
24 Oreo cookies, crushed in blender
½ cup melted butter or margarine
½ gallon ice cream, softened
1 (9-ounce) carton frozen whipped topping,
    thawed (Cool Whip)
½ ounce of Kahlúa
½ cup chopped nuts, pecans or walnuts preferred

◾ In the top of a double boiler over low heat, combine the chocolate and 2 tablespoons of butter; melt and stir together. Add the sugar, salt, and milk. Cook, stirring until thickened. Remove from heat and add vanilla; stir in well. Chill until completely cool.

◾ Combine crushed cookies with the melted butter or margarine and press into the bottom of a 9x13x2-inch pan. Spread with softened ice cream. Spread chocolate mixture on top of ice cream layer, then place in freezer until frozen.

◾ Combine the whipped topping with Kahlúa until completely blended. When the chocolate layer has frozen, spread the whipped topping mixture on top and sprinkle with nuts. Return to the freezer until frozen. Cut into 12 to 15 squares and serve.

Makes 12–15 servings.

Appalachian Brewing Company, Camp Hill, Pennsylvania

3721 Market Street
Camp Hill, PA 17011
(717) 920-BREW
www.abcbrew.com
Also in Harrisburg and Gettysburg, Pennsylvania

The Old Lee Highway, aka U.S. Route 11, runs through Camp Hill, Pennsylvania, which is located southwest of Harrisburg. US 11 is variously known as the Harrisburg Pike or the Carlisle Pike in this area and is paralleled by Interstate 81; from Camp Hill it is a short distance to Carlisle, Pennsylvania, a town famous for its classic car and motorcycle shows.

Craig DiBlasi, operations manager for Appalachian Brewing Company, gave me this recipe.

Grinnin' Grizzly Rice Pudding

1 ounce golden raisins
1 ounce dark raisins
2 ounces Appalachian Brewing Company
    Grinnin' Grizzly Spiced Ale or other
    suitable spiced ale
1½ cups cooked white rice
1½ cups milk

¼ cup granulated sugar
¼ cup light brown sugar
1 tablespoon butter
½ tablespoon vanilla extract
½ teaspoon ground cinnamon
Zest from ½ lemon

■ In a small saucepan, combine the raisins and spiced ale. Bring to a boil, remove from heat, and let steep while cooking the rice pudding. In a large saucepan, combine the cooked rice, milk, sugars, butter, and vanilla. Cook for 25 minutes or until most of the liquid is absorbed. Mix in the cinnamon, lemon zest, and drained steeped raisins. Serve warm with fresh whipped cream.

Makes 4 cups.

U.S. Route 11: The Lee Highway

U.S. Route 11, part of the numbered federal highway system created in 1925, currently runs from the Canadian border at Rouses Point in New York State to just east of New Orleans, Louisiana, for an approximate distance of 1,650 miles. For much, but not all, of the distance from Canada to Tennessee, Interstate 81 parallels US 11. I-81 ends at the junction with Interstate 40 near Dandridge, Tennessee.

The original road to bear the moniker "the Lee Highway" was a part of what was known as the National Auto Trails, which was a product of the early road-building era of the last century. As it existed then, it was a coast-to-coast route, which competed with the Lincoln Highway, as both proposed different routes from New York City to San Francisco. The Lee Highway, named for Confederate general Robert E. Lee, took a course through the South and then across the Southwest, finally going north again from San Diego through Los Angeles and on to terminate in San Francisco. Along many parts of the original route that pass through the southeastern states, the variously numbered routes are still locally known as the Lee Highway.

Like the other named roads that were promoted by private groups during the "Good Roads Movement" era, the Lee Highway's route was chopped up in 1925 when the federal highway system was created, resulting in the original route being designated with over a dozen "federal route numbers." These ranged from U.S. Route 1 between New York City and Washington, D.C., to the famous U.S. Route 101 or the Pacific Coast Highway (PCH), which runs from Los Angeles, California, to Olympia, Washington. It is interesting to note that while not as famous or the subject of research and books like the Lincoln Highway, the original Lee Highway route actually contains the easternmost and westernmost of the federal numbered highways. Ironic if you consider the Lee Highway in a way binds the union together more than the Lincoln Highway. What would the highways' namesakes think of that?

The Virginia General Assembly officially designated the section of U.S. Route 11 in Virginia as the Lee Highway in 1926. It is the section in Virginia and through to the Knoxville area of eastern Tennessee that resonates deeply with me. The Lee Highway was the primary "old road" of my childhood travels; while we also traveled the many other old roads that intersect it, US 11 was the main-line route. As I traveled along that road in the early 1960s through when Interstate 81 was completed in December 1971, my love of the road and wanderlust was developed. It was along the tapestry of intertwining roads my childhood family vacations traveled that I developed my taste for road food, my enjoyment of sightseeing, and the need to see what was over the next rise of asphalt. In a way it was because of US 11—the Lee Highway—and the people and places along it that this book is in your hands.

The Farmer's Daughter, Chuckey, Tennessee

7700 Erwin Highway
Chuckey, TN 37641
(423) 257-4650
www.thefarmersdaughterrestaurant.com

Here is an old-timey Southern dessert. The origins of the name are not clear, making for a nice culinary mystery. That you'll want a second slice is no mystery at all, because it is delicious. Try it at home or visit Dan and Rachel Tyson at the Farmer's Daughter in Chuckey, Tennessee.

Chess Pie

½ cup butter, softened
1½ cups sugar
1 teaspoon cornmeal
1 teaspoon vinegar
1 teaspoon vanilla extract
3 eggs
1 unbaked 9-inch pie shell

▪ Preheat oven to 425°F.

▪ Cream butter and sugar in medium mixing bowl until fluffy. Add cornmeal, vinegar, and vanilla. Mix well. Beat in eggs one at a time. Pour into pie shell. Bake at 425 for 10 minutes. Reduce heat to 375 and bake for an additional 25 minutes.

Makes 1 (9-inch) pie.

Amish Acres, Nappanee, Indiana

1600 West Market Street
Nappanee, IN 46550
(574) 773-4188 or (800) 800-4942
www.amishacres.com

Here is an excerpt from the *Amish Acres Recipes Cookbook* (Nappanee, Indiana, 2001):

"Within a year of the arrival of the first Quakers from England to establish Philadelphia, Pennsylvania, Mennonites settled in nearby Germantown. The Mennonites and related Anabaptist sects became known as the Pennsylvania Dutch. The farmers' market in Lancaster was established in perpetuity by royal charter of George II in 1742. Rudyard Kipling was inspired to write that the Pennsylvania Dutch lived 'as peaceful as Heaven might be if they farmed there.' Whether these Germans invented fruit pies remains possible but unanswered. There is full agreement that shoofly pie, in its original form, that of a sponge cake baked in a crust, came from Pennsylvania Dutch ovens. The heavy molasses filling made it the sweetest pie cooling on the windowsill. Its popularity among the flies being shooed from it was, possibly, the source of its name."

- -

Shoofly Pie

1¼ cups flour
½ cup brown sugar
½ teaspoon cinnamon
¼ teaspoon salt
3 tablespoons vegetable oil
½ teaspoon baking soda

¾ cup boiling water
½ cup dark corn syrup
¼ cup light molasses
1 large egg, well beaten
1 (9-inch) unbaked pie shell

■ Pre-heat oven to 375°F.

■ Combine flour, sugar, cinnamon, and salt. Blend in oil; set aside.

Dissolve baking soda in boiling water. Stir in corn syrup and molasses. Let mixture cool. Add egg.

Sprinkle ½ cup of the flour mixture into the unbaked pastry shell. Carefully cover with liquid filling. Top with remaining flour mixture. Bake for 25–30 minutes or until the mixture sets.

Makes 1 pie.

The Time Warp Tea Room, Knoxville, Tennessee

1209 North Central Street
Knoxville, TN 37917
(865) 524-1155
www.timewarpvmc.org

Here is a simple yet luscious cookie recipe that is a Time Warp Tea Room original. Next time you are traveling through the Knoxville, Tennessee, area, plan some time to visit this unique motorcycle-rider–focused eatery. They are not far from where Interstates 40 and 275 connect, so drop out of superslab warp speed and enjoy the time warp with your fellow riders.

Time Warp Tea Room Easy Cookie Recipe

1 (18.5-ounce) package devil's food cake mix (without pudding)
½ cup vegetable oil
2 large eggs, beaten
½ cup chopped pecans
3 packages individual serving size instant brown sugar and maple oatmeal

Preheat oven to 350°F.

■ In a large mixing bowl, combine the cake mix, oil, and eggs; mix until smooth. Add the pecans and oatmeal and mix until smooth. Drop teaspoons of batter 2 inches apart on ungreased cookie sheets and bake for 10 minutes. Allow to cool before serving.

Makes 24–36 cookies.

Shady Maple Smorgasbord, East Earl, Pennsylvania

129 Toddy Drive
East Earl, PA 17519
(717) 354-8222
www.shady-maple.com

When my friend Myrrh Davis from BMW Motorcycles North America recommended the Shady Maple Smorgasbord she said: "In true Pennsylvania Dutch tradition, here is a wonderful place that will stuff the biggest eater to the gills." That is one of the reasons I and many of my friends from back in my New Jersey days would ride out in to the Pennsylvania Dutch areas of the keystone state—to sample the wonderful Smorgasbord and country-style restaurants. Wholesome farm-fresh foods, served in generous quantities at fair prices by people who care about their customers and are still in touch with where food comes from. It don't get much better. So, if you are fixin' to fill yourself to the gills try starting with dessert as in this yummy Banana Cream Cheesecake.

Banana Cream Cheesecake

1¾ cups crushed graham crackers
¼ cup sugar
½ cup melted butter
8 ounces softened cream cheese
¾ cups sugar

7 cups frozen whipped topping, thawed
4 medium and firm bananas, sliced
1¾ cups cold milk
½ cup instant banana cream
    pudding mix

In a small bowl, combine cracker crumbs and sugar; stir in butter. Set aside ½ cup of mixture for topping. Press remaining crumb mixture onto the bottom of a 9x13x2 pan. In a mixing bowl, beat cream cheese and sugar until smooth. Fold in 2 cups of the whipped topping. Arrange the banana slices in crust; top with cream cheese mixture. In a bowl, beat milk and pudding mix until smooth; fold in remaining whipped topping. Pour over the cream cheese layer. Sprinkle with reserved crumb mixture.

Makes 1 cheesecake.

The Shady Maple Smorgasbord has a great history of family work ethic, customer service, and business growth, starting prior to 1970 as an IGA (Independent Grocers Alliance) roadside produce stand and growing through the years. Fast forward to the present and they are a world-class farm market, Smorgasbord, "fast food Dutchette," gift shop and more. I encourage you to check out their history on their Web site, and the travel directions so you can go and try their great foods first hand. Between now and when you visit them, enjoy this tasty dessert.

Baked Pineapple Filling

1 (20-ounce) can crushed pineapple
2 cups bread cubes
1 cup sugar
¼ cup melted butter
7 eggs, beaten

Preheat oven to 350°F.

In a large mixing bowl combine the pineapple, bread, sugar, butter and eggs, and mix together well. Transfer to a 9x13x2-inch greased pan and bake for 1 hour.

Makes 12 servings.

11

Home Sweet Home

Every trip begins and ends at home. No matter how exciting the journey is, at some point home always tugs at your heartstrings. For those like myself, who make a living traveling, we know that life on the road is not all it appears to be to the officebound. To the nontraveler it all looks so glamorous—hotels, restaurants, new sights, and interesting people to meet. All of those things are great. Yet travel is also filled with delays, bad weather, and most everything that Murphy's Law can throw at you. While I wouldn't trade my job for another, the many months I travel each year have taught me a few things.

There is no place like home sweet home, sleeping in my own bed, the joy my dogs express when I return, and, best of all, being with family. The way my travel schedule often works, I am able to get home just in time for Sunday dinner. This weekly meal is always special. We all gather together, and everyone either brings something or we team-cook at one house or another. While we enjoy a variety of dishes, especially while our several gardens are producing, we do have some special favorites.

Here are a few of those cherished recipes. I hope you enjoy them as much as we do!

This is truly a favorite for our clan; it is my father-in-law's original recipe that is often served at Sunday family gatherings. While Pop can still cook it, as he is approaching his eighty-first birthday, the cooking duty and recipe has been passed to his son Steven. I have been known to adjust my flights home from road show trips to get to the house just in time for this cheesy, delicious treat. Pop would tell you that you need to use a good sharp cheddar and grate it fresh from the block—none of that bag-o-cheese stuff will do. The recipe does not use milk, so it delivers a flavor and texture that is different from other wimpy mac-and-cheese recipes. This is such a time-honored recipe in my family that there is a special pot reserved just for making it. I know, since I got caught cooking greens in that pot. Won't do that again! Seriously, try this recipe, and it will become one of your favorite homecoming treats.

Pop Senn's Macaroni and Cheese

1 rounded tablespoon salt
2 tablespoons canola oil
1 pound vermicelli noodles, broken into small pieces
1½ pounds sharp cheddar cheese
4–6 tablespoons margarine or butter

Fill a 4- to 6-quart saucepan three-quarters full of water and bring to a boil over a high heat. Add the salt, oil, and noodles and cook for 10 minutes, stirring frequently. While the noodles are cooking, grate the cheese; set aside until noodles are done. Drain water from the noodles and return to the pot over a low heat. Add the margarine or butter and stir until melted. Then gradually stir in the cheese until all of it is added and melted. Serve immediately, or it can be reheated in the microwave later. It is also very good baked with sliced tomato and more grated cheese on top.

Makes 4–6 servings.

My lovely wife Mary and I both love to garden. We have a large organic garden in our backyard that yields fresh vegetables all summer long. This recipe is one of the simple and delightful dishes that we often enjoy during our summer Sunday family dinners and all through the week when the squash is coming in. It is always best to pick the squash when they are still small and very tender about 6 to 8 inches in length. This keeps the seeds small and tender and the skin soft, you may use store bought (picked for the same qualities) but garden fresh is always best.

The seasoning is kept to a minimum so the fresh flavor comes through. Foods like this always remind me of my summers on Mammaw's farm. There is just nothing on a plate that is better than foods so fresh that they are only minutes from picking to the stove.

Mary's Garden Fresh Yellow Squash

2 pounds yellow summer squash, sliced
1 large onion, quartered and sliced
¼ cup butter (½ stick)
½ cup water
1 teaspoon Lawry's Seasoned Salt
Shredded cheddar cheese (optional)

In a medium sauce pot combine the squash, onion, butter, water and Lawry's Seasoned Salt; cover and place over medium heat. Bring to a boil and reduce heat to low and simmer for 15 to 20 minutes until the squash is tender, stirring occasionally. Drain and serve immediately. As an option you may cover with shredded cheddar cheese.

Makes 4–6 servings.

My sister-in-law Kathie and her daughter Kimberly usually make this sweet treat of a recipe at family holiday gatherings. Kathie told me, "This recipe was given to me from Kim's grandmother Mimi when Kim was about two years old, and so it's been in the family for over twenty years. It is easy to make and makes a good-for-you yummy dessert. I leave skin on the apples, and I prefer Granny Smiths because they are firm. The recipe easily doubles or triples. I am flattered you would use this in your cookbook—thanks!"

Kathie Capps's Cranberry Apple Casserole

3 cups chopped apples
2 cups fresh cranberries
½ cup plus 2 tablespoons all-purpose flour
1 cup sugar
Butter-flavored cooking spray
3 (1⅝-ounce) packages instant oatmeal (maple and brown sugar flavor or cinnamon roll)
¾ cup chopped pecans
½ cup firmly packed brown sugar
½ cup melted butter
Pecan halves (optional garnish)

Preheat oven to 350°F.

In a large mixing bowl, combine the apples, cranberries, and 2 tablespoons of the flour; toss well to coat. Add sugar and mix well. Transfer to a 2-quart casserole that has been lightly greased with cooking spray.

In a large mixing bowl, combine the remaining ½ cup of flour, oatmeal, chopped pecans, brown sugar, and melted butter and stir well. Spoon the mixture on top of the fruit. Bake uncovered for 45 minutes. If you want, you can garnish with pecan halves.

Makes 6–8 servings.

I love macaroni and cheese, it also a family favorite, in its milder versions loved by all of us. But of course I am known for my love of hot and spicy foods, and several other members of our family are so inclined. This recipe is a fired-up macaroni and cheese recipe that I devised to provide an illuminating yet creamy cheesy treat for your fiery palettes.

I like to make this one after returning from a road trip that offered few fiery hot meals or when we are gathering for our weekly Sunday family dinners. I hope you enjoy it as much as we do.

I have used cream cheese to give it an extra rich flavor and mouthfeel, oh so creamy, and then the chipotle peppers adds just the right amount of heat to excite but not overwhelm your taste buds.

Mac Attack

2 tablespoons butter
1 medium onion, julienne
1 tablespoon chopped garlic
2 chipotle peppers packed in adobo sauce, minced
1 pound Rotini pasta, cooked al dente according to package directions
3 ounces of cream cheese, softened
2 cups shredded cheddar cheese
1 teaspoon salt
1 teaspoon black pepper

▪ In a medium sauté pan over medium-high heat, melt the butter; add the onion and sauté for 5 to 7 minutes until the onion is golden brown. Add the garlic and chipotle peppers and reduce the heat to low; simmer for about 2 minutes, stirring often and using care to not burn the garlic as it may become bitter. The pasta should be cooked during this time so that it is drained and still hot when the sauté is finished.

▪ Return the drained pasta to its pot, add the sauté, and toss together well. Add the cream cheese, cheddar cheese, salt, and pepper, and stir well until all the cheese is melted and the pasta is evenly coated. Serve immediately.

Makes 6–8 servings.

Memaw was my wife Mary's mom, Laura May Senn. She was a great lady of the South who reminded me of both my mom and my Mammaw. Sadly, she passed away just before Thanksgiving in 2007. Our whole family and all who knew her miss her dearly.

From the first time we met she accepted me as one of her own. This is an honor I will always be proud of. Having always felt that I lost my mom way too soon, Memaw was an answered prayer. I guess you could say I got to come home again.

Once she knew that I was a vegetarian, she was ever vigilant to make sure that there was something special for me at Sunday dinners. She also took great care to make things differently for me if they could be made meat-free. Memaw watched out for me, which included great care that even the utensils that touch meat did not touch things that were vegetarian. It is hard not to cry when I think of the great kindness and love that she showed me, which was her way to treat the world as well. I am most thankful for the time I was blessed to know her and always will be.

This recipe represents one of my favorites from the many things she cooked. It was adjusted from a bacon and cheese recipe that the whole family loved. Imagine how special it felt to have a quiche special made for you. Of course everyone else in the family always enjoyed it too. We would all be honored if you try this recipe and share it with the family and friends you love.

Memaw's Quiche

1 (10-ounce) package frozen chopped spinach, or
1 (10-ounce) package frozen chopped broccoli
4 large eggs, beaten
2 cups whole milk
2 cups shredded cheddar cheese (freshly shredded white cheddar is our preference)
¼ cup minced onion
¼ teaspoon salt
¼ teaspoon white pepper (optional)
1 (9-inch) frozen deep dish piecrust, thawed but unbaked

▨ Preheat oven to 400°F.

▨ Place the spinach or broccoli in a microwave bowl and cook according to package directions. Allow to cool to room temperature and to drain completely (the spinach may need to be pressed or squeezed to remove excess moisture).

▨ In a large mixing bowl combine the eggs and milk and beat with a wire whisk until just blended. Add the spinach or broccoli, 1 cup of the cheese, onion, salt, and white pepper if desired, and stir together well. Pour the mixture into the pie crust and sprinkle the remaining 1 cup of cheese on top.

▨ Bake in on the middle rack of the oven for 35 to 45 minutes or until a fork inserted into the center comes out clean and the top has lightly browned.

▨ Allow to cool for about 5 minutes before slicing and serving. Enjoy!

▨ Note: You may use spinach or broccoli, or you may want to make one of each as they are so tasty that second helpings are guaranteed to be desired. Memaw did not enjoy pepper of any kind. I have indicated it as optional since I and several others in the family enjoy it. White pepper seems to have more zing than black, but it is used so as to avoid the black flecks in the creamy-looking quiche.

Makes 1 (9-inch) pie.

- -

Our holiday-season meals would not be complete without this generations-old family recipe. Teto was the affectionate name for Sara Synder, who was Laura May Senn's mom, who was in turn my sweetheart, Mary's, mom. I never got to meet Mary's maternal grandmother, Teto. But around the family table I heard a lot about her, and I enjoyed many great down-home dishes that were her recipes. The tradition of passing down family recipes is the tradition of our personal histories; as you have seen in other recipes in this book, it happens in road food, too. While our nation is sometimes overly obsessed with youth and all things new, when it comes to returning home from an adventure, I will always take a slice of history on my plate. Save your family recipes—as they say, "you are what you eat," and if so, then within those family recipes is from whence you came.

Teto's Pumpkin Pie

2 large eggs, slightly beaten
1½ cups canned pumpkin
1 cup sugar
½ teaspoon salt
1 teaspoon ground cinnamon
¼ teaspoon ground ginger
¼ teaspoon ground cloves
¼ teaspoon ground nutmeg
1⅔ cups (1 can) undiluted evaporated milk
1 (9-inch) piecrust

■ **Preheat oven to 425°F.**

■ **Using a stand mixer with a large bowl at a low speed, combine the eggs, pumpkin, sugar, salt, and spices and mix until smooth. Gradually add the evaporated milk while continuing to mix. Pour the filling mixture into the piecrust. Bake for 15 minutes. Reduce the oven heat to 350°F and continue to bake for approximately 40 minutes. Cool before serving.**

Makes 1 (9-inch) pie.

These deviled eggs were a favorite of Mary's mom; Memaw loved them simple and fresh just the way she taught Mary to make them. They are a simple southern Sunday treat.

Mary's Delish Deviled Eggs

12 extra large eggs, hardboiled and peeled
¾ cup real mayonnaise
Lawry's Seasoned Salt

Slice eggs in half lengthwise, remove the yolks and set whites aside being careful to not tear them. Place the yolks in a medium bowl and mash with a fork until completely crumbled. Add the mayonnaise and stir until well blended. Using a small cake icing bag with a star tip, pipe the egg yolk mixture into the egg halves. Sprinkle lightly with Lawry's Seasoned Salt. Enjoy!

Makes 24 deviled eggs.

A lot of times when Mary was making her deviled eggs I would wander into the kitchen being the usual devilish cook that I am and offer to make some my way. So here is what I would do to bedevil some of the eggs so that my fiery food–loving brothers-in-law and I would have our own Sunday treat. Basically I would just use up some of the hardboiled eggs that Mary so kindly cooked and peeled. She must love me since getting those eggs peeled and ready to go is not one of her favorite chores.

Bill's Bedeviled Eggs

6 extra large eggs, hardboiled and peeled
1 teaspoon mustard
3 tablespoons ranch dressing
1 teaspoon hot sauce

½ teaspoon ground cumin
½ teaspoon salt
½ teaspoon black pepper
Paprika

■ Note: I like my eggs with a lot of salt and black pepper; I also enjoy the taste and aroma of cumin. You might wish to start with a ¼ teaspoon of each of these three seasonings and taste it first. Also if you have any leftovers—we rarely do—they make a great egg salad sandwich; just mash them up and spread between two slices of bread, and instant lunch.

■ Slice eggs in half lengthwise, remove the yolks and set whites aside being careful to not tear them. Place the yolks in a small bowl and mash with a fork until completely crumbled. Add the mustard, ranch dressing, hot sauce, cumin, salt, and pepper and stir until well blended. Using a spoon, divide the egg yolk mixture into the egg halves, and sprinkle lightly with a line of paprika to identify them as fiery. Enjoy!

Makes 12 bedeviled eggs.

My brother-in-law Steve makes this hearty soup for us from time to time. This is a great soup for a crisp fall day, especially when the day's chores include chopping a cord or more of wood, or raking the leaves from the giant oaks on Senn hill. If you serve it along with a grilled cheese sandwich you have a simple yet hearty meal. In fact we enjoy it so much that it is no longer just a cold-season treat—it is a four-season soup. Try it after a cool fall ride and I bet you will also make it all through the seasons.

Steve Senn's Black Bean Soup

2–3 tablespoons of extra virgin olive oil
1 cup sliced celery
1 cup minced onions
1 (14.5-ounce) can of cooked carrots (you may use fresh but takes more time)
1 (11-ounce) can Mexican corn
2 (10-ounce) cans diced tomatoes and green chilies
3 (15-ounce) cans black beans
Salt and pepper to taste
Sour cream

In a large soup pot heat the olive oil over medium heat, add the celery and onions, and sauté for about 15 minutes or until tender. Add the cooked carrots, corn, tomatoes and chilies, and black beans. Bring to a boil, then reduce to low and a simmer for at least 30 minutes. Add salt and pepper to taste. Serve with a healthy dollop of sour cream.

Makes 8–10 servings.

12

Travel Trailer: Extra Recipes from the Road

Seems like every time I pack my motorcycle for a trip, I always want to bring more stuff than I have room for. The bag liners simply refuse to be crammed into the hard bags. I then have to unpack everything and decide what to leave behind. Then I double check that I haven't forgotten something critical—like rain gear. It is a back-and-forth process each time. One would think that after decades of doing this I would have it down to a science. It doesn't work like that, at least for me. I am always updating gear, sometimes replacing worn or obsolete things, and other times just adding some new goodie that promised to make my road life better. So what goes and where it is packed always changes. There is, of course, a seasonal change of gear and changes according to what length trip I am planning. Some folks have solved this problem by towing a small travel trailer behind the bike. Then they can bring everything—think *kitchen sink*. In all of that packing, a wise biker leaves some room for souvenir T-shirts, beer mugs, and other road memories that one will invariably collect along the way.

Well, for me this problem of too much to pack and where it is best packed not only applies to motorcycle touring, but also to the books I write. So it never fails that there are some recipes that I feel just must be in the book, but they don't neatly fit in any particular chapter. Therefore, here is my Travel Trailer chapter, filled with extra recipes that just needed to be here. I hope you enjoy them, since I packed them just for you.

The Red Planet Diner, Sedona, Arizona

1655 W Highway 89A
Sedona, AZ 86336
(928) 282-6070

This simple but tasty dressing is served on the Solar Salad at the Red Planet Diner in Sedona Arizona. It would make an out-of-this-world addition to any salad that you beam-up to your dinner table.

- -

Solar Dressing

Olive oil
Red wine vinaigrette
Italian seasoning
Salt

In a small covered container combine the olive oil, red wine vinaigrette, Italian seasoning, and salt to taste. Cover tightly and shake well, allow to rest for at least 1 hour before serving. Shake well just before serving.

The Old Salt, Hampton, New Hampshire

490 Lafayette Road
Hampton, NH 03842
(603) 926-8322

Here is a tasty little recipe from the Higgins family of the Old Salt restaurant. It is simple to make and a perfect addition to the Goody Cole Chicken Sandwich (see the Sandwiches and Lunch Specialties chapter). The flavor of tarragon goes wonderfully with chicken, eggs, and fish, and it has an aroma that reminds one of anise. The recipe makes just enough for use on one sandwich, which is perfect since when it's made fresh you get the most flavorful result.

Goody Cole Homemade Tarragon Mayo

A pinch finely chopped fresh tarragon leaves
2 tablespoons mayonnaise

In a small bowl, combine the tarragon and mayonnaise; whisk together well. Cover and refrigerate at least 2 hours before serving to allow the flavor of the tarragon to completely infuse the mayonnaise.

Makes 2 tablespoons.

Tony Packo's—Front Street Restaurant, Toledo, Ohio

1902 Front Street
Toledo, OH 43605
(419) 691-6054
www.tonypackos.com

This great sauce is used in the Tony Packo's Hungarian Stuffed Cabbage recipe. I have placed it here since it is so good that you might wish to use it in other dishes or on vegetables. Add a little (or a lot) of hot Hungarian paprika for a more zesty version.

Tony and Rose Packo TONY PACKO'S CAFÉ

Tony Packo's Tomato-Onion Sauce

2 small onions, chopped
1 tablespoon melted butter or
   margarine

1 (16-ounce) can tomatoes undrained
   and cut up
½ cup dairy sour cream

In a saucepan, cook the onions in melted butter or margarine until tender. Stir in tomatoes and heat through. Stir in sour cream and serve.

Makes about 3 cups of sauce.

Top of the Hill Grill, Brattleboro, Vermont

632 Putney Road
Brattleboro, VT 05301
(802) 258-9178
www.topofthehillgrill.com

This dry spice rub is part of Jon Julian's great recipe for the Top of the Hill Grill Pulled Pork. But I am sure you will find it very useful in grilling other meats.

Top of the Hill Grill Dry Rub

½ cup celery salt
½ cup paprika
garlic powder
1 tablespoon black pepper

½ tsp cayenne
1 teaspoon sugar
1 tablespoon salt

Combine ingredients and mix.

Makes 1¼ cups.

Appalachian Brewing Company, Harrisburg, Pennsylvania

50 North Cameron Street
Harrisburg, PA 17101
(717) 221-1080
www.abcbrew.com
Also in Camp Hill and Gettysburg, Pennsylvania

Craig DiBlasi, Operations Manager for the Appalachian Brewing Company, told me, "ABC Harrisburg is located in a historic downtown building built circa 1915. The lagering room portion of the brewery dates to 1890."

Besides all of the history and the scale of the establishment they serve one delicious Cheddar Beer Bread, three of my favorite food groups in one recipe. How cool is that? Just give me this bread and some butter, and I am set. Go ahead, bake it at home; make sure you have a "to-go box" for whatever else you cook, because you'll have a hard time saying no to another slice of this bread.

- -

Cheddar Beer Bread

Spray cooking oil
3 cups all-purpose flour
2 ounces granulated sugar
1 teaspoon iodized salt
1 tablespoon baking powder
2 teaspoons garlic powder
8 ounces shredded cheddar-Jack cheese
12 ounces Appalachian Brewing Company Water Gap Wheat or other suitable wheat beer
2 ounces melted butter

▨ **Preheat oven to 375°F.**

▨ **Prepare an 8-inch loaf pan by spraying with cooking oil.**

In a large mixing bowl, combine the flour, sugar, salt, baking powder, garlic, and cheddar-Jack cheese and mix thoroughly. Slowly stir in beer and mix until just combined. The batter will be thick. Spread in the loaf pan and bake until golden brown and a toothpick stuck in the center comes out clean, about 60 minutes.

Cool in the pan on a rack for 15 minutes. Remove from pan and brush with melted butter and serve immediately.

Makes 1 standard-size loaf.

Deal's Gap Motorcycle Resort, Tapoco, North Carolina

17548 Tapoco Road
Tapoco, NC 28771
(800) 889-5550 (United States and Canada only) or (828) 498-2231 (outside United States)
www.dealsgap.com

Motorcyclists and sports-car enthusiasts travel from all over the world to enjoy the asphalt roller coaster that is known as the Dragon: a road with no intersections or roadside development for 11 miles and 318 turns, known officially as U.S. Route 129 on maps. The area is also known as Deal's Gap, which crosses the Smoky Mountain Range where Tennessee and North Carolina meet along the southern end of the Great Smoky Mountain National Park. Besides being a sport motorist's mecca, it is also used by locals and logging trucks, so do enjoy it with care. On the North Carolina side of the Dragon is Deal's Gap Motorcycle Resort, a place where you will find good food and camaraderie. They also have a hotel, camping, a store, and a cafe where you can rest and feed the hunger that riding the tail of the Dragon is sure to create.

Here is a down-home Southern favorite and family recipe for Deal's Gap Slayer Corn Bread from restaurant manager Jessica Venable. She also shared her family recipe for Dragon Breath Chili (see the Barbecue, Wings, and Chili chapter). Try them both at home; they will give you a taste of the Dragon. Then, while you have the fire inside of you, pull out your maps and plan a trip to Deal's Gap—it is a must-do for all who seek truly wicked asphalt!

Deal's Gap Slayer Corn Bread

1 stick butter
2 boxes Jiffy brand corn bread mix
2 large eggs
1 (8-ounce) container sour cream
1 (8-ounce) can creamed corn

Preheat oven to 350°F.

Place the butter in a 9x9x2-inch nonstick baking dish (I prefer my 10-inch cast-iron skillet) and put it in the oven to melt.

While the butter is melting, combine the corn bread mix, eggs, sour cream, and creamed corn in a large mixing bowl. Mix together until well blended.

Carefully remove the baking dish from the oven and pour the mixture on top of the melted butter. Return it to the oven and bake for approximately 30 minutes or until brown on top. To test for doneness, insert a fork in the middle; if it comes out clean, the corn bread is done. Serve immediately—it is best if eaten warm.

Makes about 12 servings.

U.S. Route 129: Tail of the Dragon

U.S. Route 129 is what is known as a "spur route," which means it is a short road that connects with a main or "parent" highway. In this case the main/parent highway is U.S. Route 29, which runs from the north starting in Baltimore, Maryland, to the south, ending in Pensacola, Florida, for a length of 1,036 miles. US 129, the spur route, runs for 582 miles from the northern end near Knoxville, Tennessee, to its southern terminus in Chiefland, Florida. The parent and its spur meet in the Athens, Georgia, area. The two roads combined cover a total of 1,618 miles, but it is less than 1 percent of that road mileage that we are interested in.

It is the eleven miles of US 129 that pass between Tabcat Creek, Tennessee, and Deal's Gap, North Carolina, that are known as the Tail of the Dragon, or simply "The Dragon." Within that eleven miles there are 318 turns, almost twenty-nine curves per mile on average. What makes it even better is that the road follows the southern boundary of the Great Smoky Mountain National Park. Because it is along the park border, there are no crossroads and no development, hence no cross traffic. The combination of a road that travels up and down across the mountains with an almost unequaled rate of curves per mile (as far as I know) with the lack of cross traffic has made this eleven miles a motorcyclist's and sports-car enthusiast's heaven.

There is a resort at Deal's Gap on the North Carolina side where you can stay (hotel or camping) or just fuel up, get a good meal, and buy a souvenir. The area is rather remote, so remember to gas up before you get there—you may wish to ride back and forth on those eleven miles a few times before you stop to top off your tank.

This is one of those roads that started as an animal trace and was used as an Indian trail and then as a migration pathway through the desolate mountain region. For a while after the Civil War, and perhaps as late as the first years of the 1900s, it even functioned as a privately owned toll road of sorts. One curve is even named

"Toll Booth"; actually, almost every curve on this eleven miles has a name, and you can download maps (including one that shows deaths since 2000) from the Internet at www.tailofthedragon.com. It is an area with an interesting history, natural beauty, Hollywood fame (including scenes from the 1993 film *The Fugitive* starring Harrison Ford), and many other great riding roads.

At one time, this eleven miles of US 129 had a speed limit of 55 miles per hour; now it is 30 miles per hour, and that speed limit is occasionally enforced with a vengeance. Crashes along the road are both common and legendary; there is a "tree of shame" where parts of crashed vehicles hang. Many folks come to this road with the intent of slaying the dragon, and they get eaten instead. This sad and tragic reoccurrence of accident, injury, and loss of life is probably the driving reason for the periodically highly enhanced enforcement of traffic laws and the lowering of the speed limits. Having personally traversed this road many times at a very vigorous pace on both two and four wheels, I can tell you that it doesn't take much to go wrong to send you off the road and into the trees or oncoming traffic. Some of the most frightening oncoming traffic can be logging trucks or tractor trailers, which need both lanes to navigate many of the tight turns. This is a federal spur highway after all, so expect some traffic, even if the remoteness makes it mostly low volume. In the end, if you visit this road, stay focused, ride within the speed limit and your personal skills, and drive a vehicle that has good brakes and tires. Don't succumb to the temptation to try to ride as fast as the person in front of you; they may be a veteran of the Dragon, more skilled, or just more foolish. If you come up behind me or someone else who isn't as fast as you, relax and enjoy the ride. Passing on this road is like playing Russian roulette: Sooner or later you pull that trigger, and it goes bang. Follow this advice, ride or drive responsibly, and then you will return home with great memories and tales of slaying the Dragon which will be just like some fishermen's tales, except you are the one that got away.

Mrs. Rowe's Restaurant and Bakery, Staunton, Virginia

74 Rowe Road
Staunton, VA 24401
(540) 886-1833
www.mrsrowes.com

Dan Tyson from the Farmer's Daughter in Chuckey, Tennessee, recommended Mrs. Rowe's to me. His fine restaurant that serves true old-time Southern country cooking was recommended to me by Tammy Blankenship, a friend from my local ABATE/CBA (American Bikers Aimed Toward Education/Concerned Bikers Association) chapter. Do you see the theme here? It speaks to the core of this book: fellow lovers of real American down-home cooking sharing places and recipes. For more than one hundred years, travelers of our roads have enjoyed food on their journeys and either brought the recipe or the inspiration back home. Here is the story of this recipe that Mollie Bryan, author of *Mrs. Rowe's Restaurant Cookbook: A Lifetime of Recipes from the Shenandoah Valley,* shared with me:

"Spoon bread, a kind of cross between a soufflé and polenta that fills your mouth with a subtle, sweet puff of corn, was added to the menu at Rowe's in the early 1990s. From time to time, Mrs. Rowe took her children to eat at a cafeteria in Roanoke, and they loved the spoon bread. Later on, as adults working in the restaurant, they wanted to add it to the menu. Mildred Rowe's sister, Bertha, had a recipe for spoon bread soufflé, but it would not hold up to the steam table. Barbara Marshall, a cook at Rowe's, volunteered a recipe that was used in a restaurant where she used to work. They tried it, and with a few changes, the spoon bread has been a big hit with the customers. Here is the version that is being served today."

About preparing this recipe, Mollie said: "The batter can be refrigerated up to six hours before baking, but the baking time increases. Spoon bread reheats well in the microwave, although the consistency is drier."

Mrs. Rowe's Spoon Bread

4 cups milk
½ cup (1 stick) butter, plus more for the dish
1 cup yellow cornmeal
4 large eggs, lightly beaten
6 teaspoons sugar
1 tablespoon baking powder
¾ teaspoon salt

▪ Preheat the oven to 350°.

▪ Butter a large baking dish and set it aside.

▪ Heat the milk and butter in a large saucepan over medium-high heat. When the milk begins to steam, whisk in the cornmeal and cook, whisking constantly, until thoroughly mixed. Remove from the heat and let cool and thicken slightly.

▪ Whisk the eggs, sugar, baking powder, and salt together in a bowl, and then whisk the egg mixture into the cooled cornmeal mixture and mix well. Scrape the batter into the prepared baking dish and place in the oven to bake until golden brown on top, about 30 to 40 minutes. Serve hot with butter.

Makes 10 servings.

Frank Sodolak, inventor of the world famous "Chicken Fried Bacon" PAUL YEAGER CAFÉ

Sodolak's Original Country Inn, Snook, Texas

Highway 60
Snook, TX 77878
(979) 272-6002

Here is a most original recipe that was recommended to me by a friend of a friend, the exact idea behind this book—riders tell fellow riders about great places and interesting food. This is the message I got from Paul Yeager:

"Hey Billy, Beau Pacheco sent me your info and said you might be interested in a unique offering from a country steak house near College Station, Texas, in a blink-of-an-eye town named Snook: chicken-fried bacon. The place is Sodolak's Original Country Inn, Texas Size Steaks & Burgers, 'Home of the Chicken Fried Bacon.' Frank Sodolak, the owner, says he made his first chicken-fried bacon in 1991. He dips the bacon strips into the fried chicken batter and cooks them in the deep fryer. They are lighter than you would expect, though still quite rich and filling. Like all good things chicken-fried, they come with a side order of cream gravy. One of the more savory things about chicken-fried bacon is its explicit suggestion of politically incorrect unhealthiness. Everything about it says clogged arteries and overloaded heart muscles, yet you can't help wondering exactly what part's going to taste the best, and in your mind you're licking your lips. I was there around noon on a clear cool Sunday, and the place was mostly full. Frank said the week earlier it had been packed, and that people come from all over to try it. A couple of guys drove nonstop down from Chicago a couple of weeks ago, had some chicken-fried bacon, and then turned around and drove back. Let me know what your thoughts are about all this. My brother, who is also a rider, gave me your first book, and I'd be pleased if I could offer something for this one."

The world famous "Chicken Fried Bacon" PAUL YEAGER CAFÉ

Well, Paul, my thoughts are, *wow,* fantastic! I know folks will enjoy this one. So I called Frank Sodolak, and he said he would share the recipe, telling me that his son Curtis would get me the details.

After I spoke with Curtis and he sent me the details, we agreed you need to do a few things to succeed with this at home. First you must use a deep fryer, not a shallow pan. The chicken fried bacon has to be completely submerged in the oil and cooked from all sides at once.

Chicken Fried Bacon

6 uncooked bacon strips
Milk for dredging
Flour for dredging
Salt and black pepper to taste
Hot sauce

▢ **Preheat a deep fryer full of oil to 365°F.**

▢ **Dip the bacon pieces into the milk one at a time, then dredge in the flour and set aside on a plate. Repeat with each piece. If you want a thicker crust, dip each breaded piece in the milk again and dredge in the flour a second time.**

▢ **Carefully place a few pieces of breaded bacon into the deep fryer. When they float and are golden brown they are finished. Remove from the deep fryer and place on paper towels while you fry the rest. Do not crowd them in the oil, as the oil will lose temperature and they will become greasy. Serve hot with salt and pepper to taste, and hot sauce if you like. Enjoy!**

Makes 1 serving.

The Time Warp Tea Room, Knoxville, Tennessee

1209 North Central Street
Knoxville, TN 37917
(865) 524-1155
www.timewarpvmc.org

The Time Warp Tea Room in Knoxville, Tennessee, makes some great grilled sandwiches. No matter which one you enjoy, this grilling oil is part of the secret formula. Try it on your own sandwich-maker creations or on veggies on the grill. It will have you warping through time to make more.

Time Warp Seasoned Grilling Oil

1 cup olive oil
1 teaspoon garlic powder
1 teaspoon dried oregano
1 teaspoon paprika
1 teaspoon powdered onion
1 teaspoon red pepper flakes

▎ **In a small bowl, combine all ingredients and mix together well. Cover and refrigerate for at least 1 hour to allow the flavor to blend.**

Makes 1 cup grilling oil.

It has been nearly a century since Emily Post had to surrender to the reality that fine-dining rooms were not readily available along the primitive roads of 1915. She simply had to make do with cooking out. Today there are many folks who travel, and cooking out is a major part of the experience they seek. This is easily seen in the RV travel culture, whether using the fancy indoor kitchen or the grilling gear carried along. It is also very popular among motorcyclists who tour the country or attend big rallies and camp. My good friend Ron Huntley and his brothers make twice annual riding and camping trips, enjoying the road and the campfire camaraderie. Ron told me: "My brothers and I enjoy this baked chicken recipe usually on the first night of our spring and fall camping and bike rides. I use a 12-inch Dutch oven with a short rack in the bottom."

So whether you are packing the cook gear on one or several bikes or bringing a chuck wagon's worth of gear while RVing, here is one for the road.

Huntley Brothers' Crossroads Cornish Hens

26 charcoal briquettes
½ teaspoon salt
¼ teaspoon black pepper
4 fresh Rock Cornish hens
1 medium onion, peeled and quartered

Light the charcoal briquettes and burn to red hot while you prepare the hens.

Sprinkle the salt and pepper onto the hens and rub in well. Insert a quarter slice of onion into the cavity of each hen. Place the hens on the rack within the pot and cover with the lid.

Place 12 of the briquettes in a circle on the lid and place the Dutch oven on top of the remaining 14 briquettes. Never place briquettes inside the Dutch oven; also never place a briquette on the center of the lid or directly under the center of the oven, as it will cause it to burn. Bake approximately 60 to 90 minutes, or until the hens are cooked completely, turning the lid every 15 minutes.

Makes 4 servings.

Here is a camping recipe from my friend and fellow moto-journalist Joshua Placa. He is the editor of jpBLVD.com and jpBLVD.com/blog; motorcycle sites dedicated to making the world a better place for bikers. He also offers guided motorcycle tours of the Indian lands and natural wonders of the Southwest through WildWindMCTours.com—ride with him and he just might cook these burgers for you while regaling you with stories from his grandpa and his own stories from years wandering the southwestern desert. He can be reached at joshua1@npgcable. com.

Josh told me this about his grandpa's burgers. "You may think there are no buffalos in Sicily, but according to Grandpa he saw one roaming the nearby hills outside Palermo, roped it, ate it. Delicious. Then again, it might have been a goat."

Joshua Placa's Grandpa's Sicilian Buffalo Burgers

1 pound ground buffalo (turkey, beef, or goat can be substituted)
Piles of herbs:
3 heaping tablespoons chopped or powdered garlic
3 heaping tablespoons chopped or powdered onion
1 teaspoon rosemary (ground in your palm to itty bitty twigs)
1 heaping teaspoon cracked pepper
2 teaspoons sea salt
2 heaping tablespoons ground ginger
3 heaping tablespoons parsley flakes
1 large egg
½ cup breadcrumbs
¼ cup wheat germ (optional)

Add all ingredients together in large mixing bowl. Mash together with big wooden spoon or better yet, your bare hand. Mush into patties. Grill over a campfire.

Makes four big healthy burgers, about two servings.

13

Biker Billy's Guide to Eating for the Long Road

Food and motorcycles: These are two very important things in my life. As you probably know, I write motorcycle cookbooks. Based on that, you might assume that the previous statement was about my work. While that would be a fair guess, there is another relationship between food and motorcycles that I want to address. How does the food you eat affect your safety as a rider? We are all aware that the consumption of alcohol, even in small amounts, will diminish our ability to ride safely. But most of us never consider that what is on our plates might have an impact on our alertness and ability to safely ride a motorcycle.

While the issues that come into play in how foods affect your alertness do have an impact on short-distance riders, it is most dramatic during long days on the road. Maintaining alertness while hammering down hundreds of miles of interstate a day can be a challenge. Your dietary intake will either enhance your alertness or undermine it. However, it is important to state that food choices alone will not keep you alert if you have other major factors working against you. Before delving into rider-friendly road foods, let's clear the table, so to speak, of those other issues.

Riding a motorcycle is a complex task that requires skills, knowledge, practice, a clear mind, and a well-rested body. The first major factor that will undermine your ability to remain alert while riding is sleep—or more precisely, lack of sleep. We all have spent the long days of fun in the sun followed by party-hearty nights at rallies like Daytona and Sturgis, each

day shortchanging sleep for fun. After a few days of this, we have developed a sleep deficit. Before that long ride home, you should pay back that deficit. Try to make it a point to get two full nights of sleep before you start your ride home. This is based on studies of fatigue in commercial truck drivers and how it affects safety performance. The essence of this is that the first night you restore most of your sleep deficit. Then, with a restful day off the road and another good night's sleep, you are good for the road. This would make a good habit both for rallying and for those extended motorcycle tours we all dream of. In that case, ride for five days and chill for two. For those of you who trailer your bike to events, this is also good advice, since it is easier to fall asleep in those comfy bucket seats than in the saddle. The next thing to be clear about is that no amount of good sleep and proper nutrition will make it safe to ride under the influence of alcohol or drugs. This includes both prescription and over-the-counter drugs. Simply put, ride straight!

With those important understandings accepted, let's look at how the foods that you eat affect riding your motorcycle safely. Motorcycling is an activity that depends on a lot of mental functions; consider the Motorcycle Safety Foundation (MSF) training technique call SIPDE, which means Scan, Identify, Predict, Decide, Execute. These are all mind-based functions. So how does your food affect your mind? The answer lies in neurotransmitters, which are the chemicals created by your brain and other organs that your brain uses to process thoughts and send and receive messages. The neurotransmitters of interest to us fall into two categories. First are the ones that support mental alertness, those being dopamine, norepinephrine, and adrenaline. Secondarily is the one that calms, soothes, or supports sleep, called serotonin. Don't run out and look for some supplement that is loaded with alertness chemicals, since taking them in concentrated form would probably have unexpected results or be downright dangerous to your health. The goal is to eat foods that will promote the appropriate mental state at the right time.

In order to make wise choices in road foods, we need to have a better understanding of how certain foods promote the production of neurotransmitters both for alertness and sleepiness. Your body, building from the nutrients in the foods you eat, produces neurotransmitters. All foods contain a variety of different nutrients, from macronutrients like proteins to micronutrients like minerals and vitamins. Thankfully, we need only focus on two key types of macronutrients, which are pretty easy to identify. Those are proteins and carbohydrates. With all the attention that the popular Atkins diet has generated, most Americans are keenly aware of carbohydrates and proteins. By balancing and timing your intake of proteins and carbohydrates, you will be able to stay more alert on the road and still be able to fall asleep at night.

Proteins are composed of complex arrays of amino acids, which are the precursors of neurotransmitters. The amino acids tyrosine and phenylalanine are involved in the development of dopamine, norepinephrine, and adrenaline, the neurotransmitters that promote alertness. The amino acid tryptophan is the precursor to serotonin, the neurotransmitter that calms and relaxes you. All three of these amino acids, in varying amounts, are in proteins. The critical issues with these amino acids are which ones and how quickly your body uptakes them. Of the three, tryptophan is usually the slowest to be absorbed through the blood-brain barrier. Since proteins are the source of the precursors for both alertness and sleepiness, how can we control the results? And where do carbohydrates enter the equation?

When you consume carbohydrates your body converts them into sugars, which are then carried through your bloodstream as the fuel that then runs your cells. Sugars give you a quick boost of energy. The simpler the carbohydrate, the faster you get the sugar rush. When the level of sugar in your bloodstream rises above the narrow range that your body likes, your pancreas will produce insulin to regulate your blood sugar (glucose) level. The insulin has the effect of driving the glucose from your bloodstream into your muscle and fat cells. It also will do the same to the amino acids tyrosine and phenylalanine, the precursors for neurotransmitters that promote alertness. Thus, carbohydrates have the effect of reducing the neurotransmitters that keep you alert, but it gets even worse. While tryptophan, the amino acid that makes you sleepy, is usually the slowest to be absorbed through the blood-brain barrier, it no longer has to compete with the other amino acids. It rapidly moves right in and makes you sleepy.

So that is the mechanics of how the two macronutrients, protein and carbohydrates, can make you feel alert or sleepy. Now let's examine how you can apply that to what you order at that roadside cafe.

On the surface it would seem that if a little protein were good, then a lot of protein would be better, and that all carbohydrates are bad. Neither is quite true. Consuming a modest amount of protein will tend to give you a mental pick-me-up; however, a large serving will, in fact, have the opposite effect, making you feel sleepy. (More on this in a moment.) While adding carbohydrates to that protein will trigger the insulin cycle already described, there are some carbohydrates that are actually helpful in maintaining alertness. With carbohydrates, the speed at which your body converts them to glucose is directly related to whether they are simple or complex. Simple carbohydrates are converted faster; the best example would be refined white sugar, which will rush into your bloodstream. Complex carbohydrates, which retain their natural fiber content, are converted more slowly, and therefore it takes more time for the glucose to enter your bloodstream. So complex carbohydrates will give you a long-lasting supply of energy while having a lower negative impact on alertness.

Now back to that large meal of proteins and why it makes you sleepy. Your body does convert protein, fat, and carbohydrates into glucose, so a large portion of protein or high-fat protein will create a rise in blood glucose levels and result in creation of more serotonin.

Simply put, a heavy meal will make you sleepy, and the more carbohydrates that are in that meal, the sleepier you will get. Heavy meals also make your body work harder to digest them. Low-fat proteins are the best for alertness.

There are two other issues I would like to address before I make some recommendations on road food. First is caffeine—it does offer some stimulation and can be helpful in temporarily boosting your alertness, but it is not a substitute for good nutrition or especially for sleep. Caffeine can take hours to metabolize and can disrupt sleep for some folks, so be knowledgeable about how it affects you. It would be better to find that motel earlier and get a solid night's sleep and an early start on the next day than to load up on caffeine to ride a few more hours and start the next day with a sleep deficit. The second issue is not food related, but it has to do with your body's natural clock. Most of us have low ebbs of energy twice a day: once in the early-morning hours when we are normally asleep and once in the late afternoon at "siesta time." It would be better to plan a rest stop during that late-afternoon lull, enjoy a meal, stretch your legs, and break the highway hypnosis. Now on to some road food recommendations.

Starting with breakfast, I would have eggs and some high-fiber cereal like oatmeal, skipping the brown sugar and raisins. Even better than the oatmeal would be oat bran, which tastes almost the same but has more fiber. High-fiber cold cereals would be good, too. Things to avoid would be simple carbohydrates like pancakes with loads of syrup, Danishes, low-fiber muffins or toast, jellies and jams, potatoes, or any major simple carbohydrates. If you eat meat, breakfast meats would be okay; lower fat is always better (though not too likely in these items). Just remember, a modest amount of protein is better than too much. A reasonably hearty but not heavy breakfast will fuel you well into the day. If you start off with a good night's sleep and add the fact that the first few hours of any trip are always a bit more exciting than the last few hours, you should be plenty alert. Besides, any coffee or tea you have with breakfast will give you a boost and demand a rest stop long before you get sleepy.

For lunch, consider a nice big salad with lots of fresh vegetables, a great source of long-release energy and fiber. Add a protein, but keep clear of the simple carbohydrates; maybe have a chef's salad. If you want a burger or dog, skip the bun and forget about the french fries. Ordering a burger without the bun has become common with the wide acceptance of the Atkins diet. If you do Mexican or Chinese, don't eat rice or noodles; these have way too many carbohydrates. I would still try to keep lunch light, especially if you stop well into the afternoon. You don't want a belly full of food just as you enter your afternoon low point.

When that afternoon low comes along, it is time to take a short break. If you tolerate caffeine well, you can consume it now so you can still fall asleep at bedtime. Enjoy a cup of joe and instead of the slice of pie that sounds so good, have a protein bar. This would be a fine time to take a short walk or stretch out those stiff muscles. Give the bike a good safety inspection, too. It is probably also the time to consider adjusting your riding gear to prepare for the cooler temperatures of evening.

Before I talk about dinner, it is important to point out that you should always drink plenty of water all day long, especially in the hotter summer months. The wind will draw a lot more moisture out of your body than you think, and hydration is critical to all body and mind functions. Also, there is no reason to not consider spreading your eating across a few smaller meals. That said, there is a benefit to your mental and physical freshness that comes from a good thirty- to forty-five-minute break after every few hours of riding. Unless you are a knowledgeable and experienced iron-butt rider, try to avoid more than ten hours of riding in one day. There is a reason why they place a limit on the number of hours a trucker can drive a day. The same biology applies to you on your bike.

I would strongly suggest that you have your dinner very near where you are staying for the night. If you need to ride any length of time after dinner, do the lunch foods again and definitely keep it light. Remember, as the day's light fades, a few dangerous things combine—dusk makes it harder to see, your body (and everyone else's) starts to move toward a slowdown, and all those nocturnal critters think it is time to cross the road. This is truly prime accident time.

What follows is a recommendation for a meal that will promote serotonin and set you up for a good night's sleep. Enjoy that heavy protein you have been lusting for and yummy things like dinner rolls and potatoes, or a nice plate of pasta with oil and garlic. A big burger with all the fixings and those french fries that sounded so tempting at lunch would be good. Treat yourself to some comfort food; it is your reward for a day of safe, alert riding. Speaking of reward, have that slice of pie or rich dessert—you deserve it. If you pick your night's stopover right, you can walk back to your room, stretching out those road legs so you will be ready for a good night's sleep and a great start on the next day of riding. Of course, if you are home now, you can just wander into the living room and go to a chair.

I should point out that I am not a registered dietician or a doctor—just a well-worn road rider. These things work for me and are based on my personal research. Each person is different. With that in mind, I suggest that you follow what works for you and the recommendations of your family doctor. Enjoy the food and ride safe!

Resources

Three of the wonderful eateries that shared their recipes and their stories did so by sending me their cookbooks and granting permission for me to reprint their recipes contained in this book. All three books are a joy to read and contain a wealth of great recipes. I am proud to have them in my home library and recommend them to you. I am sure you will enjoy them.

Blue Willow Inn Bible of Southern Cooking
(Rutledge Hill Press, 2005—ISBN 1-4016-0227-4)

Over 600 essential recipes southerners have enjoyed for generations; the most extensive collections of Southern recipes ever in one book.

Blue Willow Inn Restaurant
294 N. Cherokee Road (Ga. Highway 11)
Social Circle, Ga. 30025
Toll Free: (800) 552-8813
Phone: (770) 464-2131
Web site: www.bluewillowinn.com

Dillard House Cookbook and Mountain Guide
(The Dillard House, 1998—ISBN 1-56352-547-X)

The Dillard House cookbook is a wonderful compilation of their traditional, Southern recipes that they serve presently in their restaurant, and the book also contains intriguing mountain stories about the old days.

The Dillard House
1158 Franklin Street
Dillard, GA. 30537
Toll Free: (800) 541-0671
Phone: (706) 746-5348
Fax: (706) 746-3344
Web site: www.dillardhouse.com

The Mrs. Rowe's Restaurant Cookbook:
A Lifetime of Recipes from the Shenandoah Valley
(Ten Speed Press, 2006—ISBN 1-58008-734-5)

A narrative cookbook that tells the story of a woman who grew up in the hills of Virginia on a struggling family farm. A woman who bucked the status quo—not because she wanted to—but because she needed to survive.

Mrs. Rowe's Restaurant & Bakery
74 Rowe Road
Staunton, Virginia 24401
Phone: (540) 886-1833
Web site: www.mrsrowes.com

Four dear friends of mine from the community of motorcycle riders and writers were of great help in the hunt for biker-friendly and delicious roadhouses. I highly recommend you read their stories any chance you get. If you are in publishing and need talented writers, photographers and commentators on this motorcycle life, here is their contact information.

Susan Buck
Email: susanbuck@aol.com
Susan Buck has been riding motorcycles since 1986. She served as editor of *Thunder Press East,* 1996–2000, and her words and photos have appeared in dozens of motorcycle publications. She is the recipient of the Motorcycle Riders Foundation's Thomas Paine award for outstanding written advocacy. In 2008, she edited and contributed to *Rubber Side Down: The Biker Poet Anthology*—www.bpwa.net

Beau Allen Pacheco
Phone: (949) 500-7920
Email: wobi@aol.com
Web site: www.beauallenpacheco.com
Beau Allen Pacheco, having roared through thirty-two countries, is one of the world's premier motorcycle travel journalists. His work appears in Harley-Davidson publications as well as *Cycle World Magazine,* and *American Rider Magazine.*

J. Joshua Placa
Phone: (928) 282-9293
Email: joshua1@npgcable.com
Web sites: www.jpBLVD.com; www.WildWindMCTours.com
Joshua Placa covers the motorcycle industry through his Web site, www.jpBLVD.com. He is also partnered in a motorcycle touring company, WildWind Motorcycle Tours, which offers guided programs throughout the Southwest. He is available for freelance missions.

Clement Salvadori
8240 Toloso Road
Atascadero, CA 93422
Email: salvadori@charter.net
Traveler, writer, motorcyclist and adventurer *par excellence*, and the man who has the job most bikers wish they had.

If you would like to contact Biker Billy:

Biker Billy Cooks With Fire
P.O. Box 1888
Weaverville, NC 28787
Phone: (828) 658-8130
Email: bikerbilly@bikerbilly.com
Web site: www.bikerbilly.com

Acknowledgments

Writing a book is a lot like riding a motorcycle on a long distance solo tour. You alone are at the wheel so to speak, yet you are not alone. Along with you there are a lot of folks who helped to get you out there and back home again safely. For the solo rider they are all the people who trained you to ride safely; those who designed, built and maintain your motorcycle; your family and friends who offer all sorts of support, advice and prayer; and the uncountable number of folks who, through their dreams and hard work, built the roads and all the businesses you depend on during your great riding adventure—now that is a huge network.

So it is here that I would like to thank my network. I owe a deep debt of gratitude to all the dreamers, visionaries, and risk-takers who through their efforts over the more than a hundred years of motorized travel brought forth the wonder that is the American Roadscape. Further, to the many folks whose hands did the actual work of building and maintaining the roads, vehicles, and all the businesses that serve and support our freedom to travel. And especially to our brave folks, who have in the past, currently do, and will in the future serve this great nation in our Armed Forces. They pay the price of freedom, which is never free—all that we enjoy in our free society is thanks to the freedom that they purchased for us at the most terrible price. I encourage you to take a moment to thank all our veterans at every opportunity, especially the ones who are returning home these days.

This book has been an interesting journey to write and it has presented challenges I could not have foreseen. The topic could span a library shelf and not include all the great places and recipes that the American Road Food Culture has to offer. What has evolved is different than what I first envisioned and is a better book for it, and that is due to the help of many people. Before I name names, I am sure I will miss somebody. To you my dear friend whose name is not here, thank you for your help and contribution, and please accept my humble apology.

I would like to thank my literary agent Carol Mann and her assistant Nicole Bergstrom for their steadfast and creative help in finding a home for this project. Thanks go to my publisher The Globe Pequot Press (GPP) for enthusiastically bringing this book to market. I have been blessed to work with a great team of creative folks at GPP. Heather Carreiro, my editor, has been a comfort and ally during the complex process of gathering the many fine recommendations, roadhouses and their recipes. She kept my voice and vision intact and made it better and clearer—not a simple feat to accomplish and she did it with style.

No book simply goes from an edited manuscript to the finished book you are holding without the work and creativity of many different folks, each with a different area of expertise and vision of the final product. Much like the conductor of an orchestra, Gia C. Manalio-Bonaventura, my project manager, has been the person who brought a cacophony of creativity into a harmonious whole, all in the proper timing. And thanks to assistant project manager Jess Haberman for her hard work down the homestretch. Beyond all the words there must be good art and design. A book's appeal starts with the cover; Diana Nuhn my cover designer, has done a fabulous job in designing a cover that says "come adventure with me." Then what lies between the covers must deliver the words and pictures in a way that pleases the eye while making the information easy to use. It is quite a creative challenge; three folks worked very hard and succeeded in making each page spread a joy to look at. They are, Libby Kingsbury, designer, Melissa Evarts and Casey Shain, layout artists.

Some sage once said, "Once a book is done, the real work is just begun." I would like to thank Bob Sembiante, my publicist, and Kira Savino, marketing intern for the great work we are about to do together in spreading the word about this book to every place there is a hungry traveler or armchair adventurer looking for great roadhouse food.

My evolved vision of this book was to share and inspire folks with my love for the American road, its history, and the great food and roadhouses found along those roads. I also wanted to continue the sense of building community that was a byproduct of my last book *Biker Billy's Hog Wild on a Harley Cookbook*. Since that book's publication, I have learned that almost everyone loves to share recipes and recommendations of good places to ride to and eat at. No one rider can cover all the millions of miles of road in America and eat every dish at every roadhouse in one lifetime; although many of us try, it is just one really large country and a lot of calories, not to mention time and gas money. But divide that among the millions of us that "ride to eat and eat to ride" and it is a proverbial piece of cake (believe me, even cake can still be a difficult recipe).

So many people responded with recommendations of their favorite places to visit for good food. I want to thank everyone that responded when I put the word out about this project. Not every recommendation made it in the book, I am sorry if yours was one of those. I want to send a heartfelt thanks to all the restaurateurs who took the time to share recipes and some of their personal history of feeding hungry travelers. Some I have dined with already. For the rest, I am looking forward to burning a path to your dining room.

In this gathering process I also reached out to several longtime friends and fellow travelers in the motorcycle industry. In particular I want to thank, Susan Buck, Beau Allen Pacheco, Joshua Placa, and Clement Salvadori. Over the years I have worked with, been edited by, or shared the stage or printed page with them, and in each and every case it has always been an honor and pleasure. They all are riders and commentators on this motorcycle life and connoisseurs of good roads and road food. If you ever have the chance to ride or dine with any of them, consider yourself blessed. I do.

I would also like to thank Ken Ostermann at The Harley-Davidson Motor Company for allowing me to reuse some material I wrote for them. And thanks go to Edward Batchelder who edits my syndicated monthly column, part of the "Introduction, Roads Run Through It" section.

I would like to thank my family who has endured this time of creation with me. In the book I have shared beloved recipes from them with you. Coming home and sharing meals with them is the best way to end my many road trips; I hope you my reader know that joy with your family at the end of each adventure. Very special thanks go to my sweetheart and wife Mary; she has been helpful and supportive throughout this whole process. This book was researched and written during a trying and eventful time in our lives, which included the loss of her mom, Laura May Senn, a fire that destroyed her familial home, and our wedding and honeymoon. The cover photo was taken by my niece, Stevie Senn, who along with her father, my new brother-in-law Steven Senn, spent the better part of a workday setting up a shot that would exactly fit the cover art. Thank you both. My daughter Sarah K. Nix took many of the pictures of me in this book. esides being a great cook and baker, she is a budding photographer, she is also a joy to my heart. Thank you, Sarah.

Lastly, I would like to thank a kind and loving God who has blessed me with manifold blessings!

Index

About the Author

Bill Hufnagle, aka Biker Billy (bikerbilly.com), is the host of a cable cooking show and the author of three previous cookbooks. A Harley rider who loves all things hot and spicy, he has been on *The Tonight Show with Jay Leno, Live with Regis and Kelly, Good Morning America,* and National Public Radio, and is a frequent guest at motorcycle rallies nationwide. He lives in the Blue Ridge Mountains north of Asheville, North Carolina.